Ten Years a Bohemian

Émile Goudeau

Translated By Richard Robinson

Sunny Lou Publishing Company
Portland, Oregon, USA
http://www.sunnyloupublishing.com

2nd Edition: January 1, 2024
1st Edition, Revised & Corrected: August 20, 2022
Original Publication Date: March 21, 2021

ISBN: 978-1-955392-46-4

* * *

This translation from the French of *Dix ans de bohème* is based on what appears to be the first edition from 1888, published by Lemerre, and printed (20.5.1888) by Paul Dupont, Paris. (But see the footnote that mentions Gabriel Vicaire and 1889.)

Contents

Miniscule Preface

In its September 10, 1887 issue, *The Searchers' Intermediary*[1] asked where details could be found on the *Hydropaths*. I responded at that time that very few details existed, apart from the hard-to-find *Hydropath* journal, and a leaflet by Léo Trézenick entitled *The Hirsutes*. That made me dig out, from an old cabinet, some very old papers, where I had collected the following notes, destined to serve as the basis for a much longer work on the *Hydropaths*, the *Hirsutes*, and the *Chat Noir*, when all that would have acquired the necessary patina of time and stumping of distance.

– Émile GOUDEAU.

---

[1] *The Searchers' Intermediary*: *l'Intermédiaire des chercheurs*.

Chapter One

Me, the author, I *or* we. – *The hotel with false truffles.* – *State Finances.* – *Francisque Sarcey.* – *The café-forum.* – The Renaissance *by Émile Blé-mont.* – *The poetry of Paris.*

The *me* is hateful, the *I*, perpetual, annoying; I will employ them here then as little as possible. However, to say the *author*, in the third person, becomes insupportably pretentious after a while, and to say *we* belongs to kings and bishops. How to proceed then to narrate events, big or small, that one had been one of the principal actors in? Phooey, I'll intermix the *me*, the *I*, the *we,* and *the author*, asking the readers of this book to consider that, if the *me* of others is profoundly hateful, everyone finds his own proper *me* delicious. I'm counting on that psychological reflection to gain the indulgence of the public, to whom I release these light memories of an epoch of gay Bohemianism, the last perhaps, it being understood that blackest pessimism casts a shadow today on the faces and hearts of twenty-year olds.

This has nothing to do with *pontificating,* nor with announcing to the world that a special generation is worth more than its predecessors or its successors; but to recount a little of this and that of the literary or artistic vicissitudes that comrades, over the course of the years, have been moved by and advanced, friends more or less, in various capacities, but connected by similarities in age and taste. If some critical analysis is intermixed here and there into the story, it will be that of a good child who no longer believes today that literature is a sacerdocy, and who finds it in bad taste, alas, that in the midst of the cruel indifference with which the best productions of poetry are received these days, poets are compelled very pointlessly to tear each others' head off, so much the worse since many have such fine ones, and since everyone is fond of that appendage. The literary field is not at all a municipal council where one must slit each other's throat to be able to ascend to the tribunal; there is a place for everyone.

I stop these reflections here, and I begin with *my* beginning.

I had left Gascony, my mother, – or rather, o pun! my father

Périgord[2] – with two hundred francs in pocket, plus a title to supernumerary employment with the ministry of finance, and, in the bottom of a trunk, a drama in verse, a modern comedy, and the outline
for a novel; very timid by temperament, very bold by will, you see
the provincial who could be, around 1874, your very humble servant.

As an attentive reader of *The Bohemian Life*,[3] the neophyte
Parisian sets himself up in the Latin Quarter, as tradition would have
it! It was rue de l'Ancienne-Comédie, a hotel with narrow facade,
tall mansard roof, and old through and through. Already several
comrades from high school had elected to live in that house whose
senility perspired through all its plaster pores, through all its long-s-
ince disjoined and cracked boards. Evidently that abode had stored
two centuries worth of rain, and the mold of the most ancient
regimes flourished there from before '89.[4] The memory of that wor-
m-eaten roost is intimately bound, in the memory of the parrots who
slept there, to an undefinable smell of vague mushrooms and implau-
sible truffles: ghost mushrooms! phantom truffles! out-and-out rot-
tenness! Perigordians that we were, that didn't surprise us particularly: our woods smelled the same, during the autumn downpours.

French administration struck me in a most remarkable manner. The bureau chief who received me asked me this:

"Have you been employed before?"

"No," I responded sincerely, "insofar as I'm supernumerary."

"That's too bad," said the chief in a serious tone of voice.
"Well, we'll find something for you to do."

He called one of the head clerks and gave him some instructions. That clerk led me to an office packed with editors and copy-
ists. There, he had me sit down in front of a desk, placed two large
ledgers under my nose, a red pencil in my hand, and said to me,
without smiling:

"This ledger of computation has been checked already with

---

[2] pun... Périgord: it's a pun for "père," rhyming with "Pér*," in French means father.

[3] *The Bohemian Life: La Vie de Bohème, a* novel by Henry Murger.

[4] '89: 1789; i.e., the *ancien regime*, before the Revolution.

black pencil, blue pencil, green pencil, yellow pencil; it's a matter of knowing whether the numbers have been identically entered in both ledgers; you are going to check – oh! but very attentively – with your red pencil."

From ten in the morning, until five in the evening, I checked off the previous checks. Admirable operation! To get to this point, I had studied eight years at school, received two diplomas, and took a special exam, in which I had been interrogated on administrative law, political economy, how to keep a budget, how to maintain ordinary and extraordinary resources for the State, how to deal with loans and the stock exchange, etc., etc. Moreover, inquiries were made into my moral character, and that of my family, including my ancestors. Admirable operation! for which, besides, being supernumerary, I didn't pocket a single one of those centimes, whose formidable additions I checked, to the half and quarter centime, to the sum total inscribed at the end of the ledger, that is: thirty-two billion, six hundred twenty-five million, four hundred fifty-nine thousand, eight hundred twenty-seven francs, forty-two centimes and a quarter.

In the evening, at the modest *table d'hôte* on rue Hautefeuille, where I met some comrades, I let off steam, with all the irony that my Perigordian coarseness, devoid of any Attic respect, could pour out on the administration, when one of my table companions, having previously been promoted to deputy, then general director of the ministry of foreign affairs, said to me:

"You are a cog, a very small spring, but the machine is large, superb in its entirety."

Very well, having become a cog, I resigned myself to it. However, it was not for this that I had come to Paris, but to launch verse and prose like fireballs onto an astonished world.

Only, timid to a fault, I didn't dare mention it to anyone, not even my comrades, fearing their mockery; so much so that at the end of one year, I found myself employed working in the same office, checking the same centimes, not having taken a single step towards glory nor the heavens that are aureoled with it. Timid, frightened even, I stood face to face with my drama and with my comedy. Men of letters appeared to me, at a distance, immense like twenty-cubit tall statues set fiercely on a pedestal rising three hundred meters above the pavement. I imagined that M. Leconte de Lisle's toe measured, on the ground of the Grand'Ville, one arpent at least, and that an entire army, with their weapons and baggages, could easily bivouac in the shadow of M. Théodore de Banville's pinky.

If Paris, represented at the ministry by a serious and decorated bureau chief, considered me barely capable of checking with a red pencil, in order to finalize some mediocre additions, a checking already performed in every color of the rainbow, with what presumptuousness would it not have been for me to venture upon literature, that realm where surely, at the start, I would not have been asked even to polish the boots of great men, no, but simply to look at how someone else polished them, so as to learn.

Without any doubt, the young, the debutants, already famous in the Latin Quarter, and in Montmartre, frightened me less; I felt them near and approachable, but, nevertheless, they also intimidated me.

In the evenings, leaving behind the card games of manille or polignac that my high-school buddies were fond of, I would go for a walk around Odeon towards café Voltaire or café Tabourey; through the windows, I saw the nose of a poet, the hat of a novelist, the beard of a dramaturge. Sometimes I entered on the balls of my feet, plunking myself down at a table near the door, asking for a glass of beer, in a low voice, and a journal, which assisted me in maintaining a countenance. On the sly, I cast glances at the sacred clan; – they must have taken me for a little sneak.

I returned home, discouraged by that stupid attitude, and, in order to console myself, hunkered down at my work table, to perfect the masterpiece necessary for my introduction into that ideal world, where, while drinking, instead of playing at a game of manille, one knew how to put ideas into action, like simple pawns, on the immense chessboard of poetry.

Finally, one day, like an enraged sheep, I took my timidity and threw it overboard; I was going to see – oh! not a poet, not one of those men who by vocation was on familiar terms with the gods and the stars, no – but a literary hack who appeared more approachable to me. And yet, for fear of ridicule, I brought no manuscript along: not my drama, nor my comedy, not even a sonnet; and I presented myself, weaponless, at Francisque Sarcey's place.

That was, gentlemen, a beautiful conference, at the end of which the prince of criticism declared to me that it was all a matter of chance and talent, and that, if I possessed one and the other, he, the critic, would be pleased to see my name come before his writing desk and under his quill.

Then, weary of working in the shadow of the furnished hotel, amidst the hybrid smells of truffles and mushrooms, I began to frequent literary cafés, counting on chance to help me strike up a friendship with poetic heroes, and the demigods of the sonnet.

This is the place to expand on *café life*. The old dictum: it is better to write a tragedy than to visit a café, – has become false in practice. To sit in a dark and gloomy corner and write a tragedy is the most cretinous thing to do today. The editorial offices of the theater are arch-closed to the unknown; moreover, the salons have lost much of their old influence; one must then, in a city like Paris, mix in with the crowd, get involved with people on the street, and live, like the Greeks and Latins did, on the *agora* or in the *forum*. Under the pluvious skies of Paris, the *agora* or the *forum* is the café, or, for faubourg politicians, the humble wine merchant on the corner. The cafés are the places of reunion, where, between two games of bezique or dominoes, one can hear long dissertations – sometimes confused, alas! on politics, strategy, law or medicine. What's more, these establishments have replaced the Grove of Academus,[5] the famous grove where philosophers put forward peripatetically their inductions and deductions; they take the place of the Hotel Rambouillet, where Oronte's sonnet captured the praise of both Benserade and Voiture.[6]

That is particularly true in the Latin Quarter and Montmartre.

---

[5]Grove of Academus: an olive grove outside the city of ancient Athens that philosophers frequented, including Plato. Thus the origin of the word Academy.

[6]Benserade and Voiture: Isaac de Benserade who wrote a sonnet entitled "Job" and Vincent Voiture who wrote a sonnet called "Uranie," both visitors to the salon of the marquise de Rambouillet in the 1600s.

The young men who come to study, in the scant entertaining, furnished hotels, experience a huge need for camaraderie and chit-chat
in the French fashion; they go out in search of, and find, what they
are looking for, that is to say, in extension of the Parisian street, what
is called a café. Those in particular who dream of literature, and
who, arrived from the provinces, know nobody and would not know
which of the hundred thousand doors in Paris to knock on, the poor
troubadours, thrown onto the place de la Grand'Ville, considering
themselves fortunate to go and roam about among quasi-celebrities
and demi-stars, whom one can rub elbows with in the places of reunion open to everyone.

The café becomes the branch office, or better, the antechamber of the editorial offices.

Because there is always, in the vicinity of boulevard Saint
-Michel, a literary journal, sometimes two, which sets the tone. At
that distant epoch (1874-1875), the small review charged with the
poetic destinies of the Left Bank was called *The Renaissance,* run by
the poet Émile Blémont. I read attentively that compilation wherein
the different poetic schools of the time rubbed elbows and sometimes went to cuffs, in witness whereof an article entitled "The Old
Failures," in which Jean Richepin attacks specifically some of the
collaborators of *The Renaissance*. With the intransigence of youth, it
would consider then as a true ancestor a Methuselah, an old beard, a
fossil, an over-the-hill and obsolete and smelling-of-the-coffin person, – anyone who had written under the Empire[7] and before the ca-
balistic and black year of 1870.[8] One of the poets who was attacked,
a blond Parnassian of thirty-five years, retaliated: "Failed? maybe;
but old? come on!"

Nevertheless, one felt a bit revolutionary in the clan of new-
bies, of those who came after the war; it seemed as though a ditch
had been enlarged between the two perfectly distinct epochs; one
cried death to the operetta, for the renewal of drama, for the renais-

---

[7]The Empire: the Second French Empire, when Napoleon III, the nephew of
Napoleon Bonaparte, ruled France from AD 1852-1870.

[8]1870: the end of the Second French Empire when Napoleon III was captured after
the Battle of Sedan, during the Franco-Prussian War; the Paris Commune began
shortly thereafter in 1871.

sance of poetry, for a poetry that was more alive, less shut up in the tabernacles by the pious hands of the servants of rich rhyme; one wanted to re-animate the impassive muse, give her some muscles and nerves, and see her walk, less divine, more human, among the sovereign throngs. In short! one fought by epigrammatic blows for possession of a scrap of the royal coat that Victor Hugo, like Alexander the Great, had left hanging from the croup of his hippogryph.

Naturally, from the back of my furnished hotel, I desired a corner of that purple, and, encouraged by the presence of Richepin, Gabriel Vicaire, and some others, very young at that time, among the editors of *The Renaissance*, I slipped one evening, as night was falling, into the offices of the journal, located at rue Jacob 11, in a dusty entresol, and left a piece of verse written (as you can well imagine) on a ministerial and bureaucratic sheet of paper.

When I returned to get a response, I was told that that poem didn't square with the review's *genre*. Ah! since then, when reading respectfully the verses written by Émile Blémont, I understood that we scarcely had the same genre.

After that, I fell back to my dark nights of a relentless worker.

The supernumerary position left me very poor, and damn! I sure needed a strong faith in the future, to pass the evenings, without a fire, polishing my verse, after having spent the whole day checking interminable ledgers. Youth is nice! And, to top it off, not to be disheartened when the only review of poetry that existed at that time condemned my *genre*, in the words of one of those demigods of rhyme, whom I saw now and then at the café Voltaire, inhaling demi-tasses and passing judgment on the living and the dead with a terrible and peremptory assurance.

You don't know anyone! and you want to sing? Come on, miserable Perigordian, you should know that reviews are like banquets where each one sings *his own* at dessert, and where the unknown passerby wanting do the thirteenth would be shown the door. One must be invited, for god's sake!

Also, on Sundays, walking off my lassitude of the week before, I would wander alone, trying to understand the great and solitary Paris.

And I loved it, that Paris! its streets and its boulevards, its enormous edifices, its squares, its Champs-Élysées, its small trees, its omnibuses, its fiacre stations! The colors of the sun or the gas lamps adorned each detail in that prestigious ensemble, or even the violet grayness that the cold and unctuous fog casts on the always renewed tableau, on the kaleidoscope of beings and things. And, also, I venerated the Parisian noise – the growling of storms, the murmur of forests, the plaintiveness of Oceans – that perpetually shakes the atmosphere. And, also, I adored the joy of the unexpected, the *chassé-croisé* of women in frills, the crazy window dressings, the cobblestones spread out or piled up, buildings knocked to the ground, and others built in the sky with large support frameworks, which from afar look like gigantic nets and, even farther away, like lace.

The love of Paris, with its joyful or gloomy Seine, the smoke of *bateaux-mouches* above and, below, the terrible flow of foreign objects that bang into the bridge piles.

Ah! the happy vocation of the gawking gawker, the naïve Meridional amused by the least of things, and who found more intense poetry in that than in calculated and cold elucubrations. That was, yes, some vivid poetry! But how to extract it from those gas lamps, those small trees, those yellow, green, or blue omnibuses?

"There is arsenic in the armchair of the president of assizes," said Raspail at the trial of Orfila. The only question is how to extract it.

Similarly, there is poetry everywhere.

And I returned to my cold cellule to entrust to paper things in *my genre*, extracting the arsenic from armchairs.

Chapter Two

Project of a journal for young people. – *The autographs of Victor Hugo.*
– *Adelph Froger, the* Republic of Letters. – *The* Sherry-Cobbler. – *Some
songs.* – The Living.

I made the acquaintance of some poets in a bizarre fashion. Precisely
in one of the last issues of *The Renaissance*, – that was the first journal I saw die! How many since then!! – I read the following little
note: "Poets, who would like to come to a mutual understanding in
order to found a review or journal, should address themselves to M.
M*** T***, rue L***, Friday, at eight o'clock in the evening."

I answered that call.

As eight o'clock struck, in the opaque fog of a winter
evening, more somber still in the Batignolles than anywhere else
(one never knew why), I climbed with fleet step the six floors that
separated the ground of the rue Legendre from the residence of the
beneficent man who agreed to create a journal for *young people*.

I was expecting to see some old philanthropist, some Saint
Vincent de Paul, holding a ready-made sonnet in each hand, and a
multitude of lost alexandrines and orphaned hemistiches hanging off
the sides of his dressing gown. I was imagining, in my provincial
naïvety, that, since everything can be found in Paris, I was going to
meet adoptive fathers of poor but genial works, which cluttered
drawers, those coffin-shaped cradles.

Such were my thoughts, on the landing of the first floor.

I continued my ascension. But the closer I got to the destina-
tion, I felt building in me that particular form of terror known as
stage fright, and I indulged in every sort of mimicry of hesitation,
before pronouncing *"alea jacta est!"* in the more modern form of:
"Let's go!" – I rang the bell that, in a heart beat, put an end to all my
pointless palpitations.

A well-lit salon, fitted with a large quantity of chairs. Nobody. Ah! yes! yes! in a corner, on the right, a young blond-haired

man, svelte, very smooth chinned, poorly dissimulating a profound boredom; in another corner, a dark-haired young man, small, who kept quiet as well, but sucked on the knob of his cane. Me, thus far the third, I sat in yet another corner. Bearded, very dark, with a menacing look, a bit nervous, and with a feeling of foreboding, I waited in that little desert, where the chandelier blazed over a caravan of unmoving chairs. A table in the middle of the room, with a glass, a spoon, sugar, water, in short everything that presaged a speaker. A quarter of an hour passed, then an hour. The big blond-haired fellow grumbled, the short brown-haired fellow, restless, left his chair, and, noticing the sofa, slipped into it, crossed his extended legs one over the other, and resumed sucking on his cane with a somnolent expression. Me, habituated since childhood, by destiny, to the most sordidly cruel events, I remained impassive.

I told myself *in petto*: a little correctness, my friend! the small brown-haired fellow is perhaps one of our young glories, the blond fellow is doubtless the son of some celebrity, don't budge an inch.

The two others must have had the same reflections. Happily, all things come to an end! A door opened, and a man in his thirties, tall, thin, well groomed, with the appropriate attitude, presented himself:

"I beg you to forgive me for making you wait so long, gentlemen," he said, while making a circular greeting.

Our host, – for it was him! – gained the armchair situated in front of the glass of sweetened water; he didn't cough at all, but, assuming a capable, but genial air, he began:

"I have here, gentlemen, nine letters from poets excusing themselves for being unable to attend the reunion this evening: they are MM. de Banville, Leconte de Lisle, de Bornier, Duparc, Lalune, Tartempion, etc. I will not read you their missives; but I'm anxious to share with you, before explaining to you what I mean to undertake, the superb autographed letter that our illustrious and adored master, Victor Hugo, sent to me:

"This is the time for poets. Your enterprise is noble. I am

with you... V.H."

The blond-haired and brown-haired young men began to laugh; I thought it was endearing, but what followed was going reveal what lurked at the back of their obscure thoughts.

M.T*** continued:

"There are only the three of us..."

"Four," interrupted the brown-haired fellow.

"I wasn't counting myself," rejoined M.T*** modestly. "In short, it has to do with the founding of a hebdomadary review in the best interests of poets, and the first to roll up their sleeves and pitch in would obviously be the most handsomely remunerated. But, before I reveal to you the marvelous plan I have in mind, designed to pull poetry up out of the stagnation it has fallen into, because it is in stagnation!..."

"Ah! yes," said the svelte, blond fellow.

"Yes! We must get to know each other a little."

"Absolutely," said the small brown-haired fellow.

We introduced ourselves, as best we could, each to the others: M. T***, M. Adelphe Froger, M. Edmond Nodaret, M. Émile Goudeau.

"But," added our host – and he calmly fretted over the sugar in the water with his spoon, – "but, we must present ourselves to each other *as poets*. If you have brought something with you, for example: a sonnet, an ode, triolets?..."

To this invitation, the blond Adelphe responded by drawing from his pocket a manuscript, and read some very Parnassian poems: the images, the alliterations, the rich rhymes, for the form; for the substance, a collection of pretty clouds in a tunnel. We applauded. The svelte blond fellow, triumphant, immediately exhibited a letter from Victor Hugo, which he had kept to top things off. The master had written to him: "Forever forward, and towards the light! – V.H."

Then it was Edmond Nodaret's turn, the small brown-haired

fellow. He read quasi-classical poetry: witty, a relaxed form, a debutant columnist's amusing prosaicness, which will turn out to be very
amusing later on. When he had finished, he pulled out of his portfo-
lio a letter that Victor Hugo had addressed to him and made us familiar with it: "Ossa and Pelion are nothing, one must climb Parnas-
sus; you are on your way. Keep going. – V.H."

Then it was my turn to speak. I felt cruelly humiliated before
them, the Master's elect, not having in my possession any recom-
mendation. That really crushed me! I felt abandoned, fumbling about
in the void, without a helping hand.

Nonetheless, bravely unruffled, I read a neo-Greek sonnet,
wherein I tried to express a feeling of Hellenistic atavism, so remarkable and so remarked on by the people who play baccarat.

I was equally applauded; but, – o dreadful fate! – I had no
signed letter to show. I was immediately relegated to the category of
amateur poets, people who are not on familiar terms with the stars. I
would have, perhaps, that evening, said goodbye forever to a vocation wherein one had to display a *certificate* on the door, in the style
of *medalists* from School of Fine Arts, if by happy chance, M. T***,
our host, hadn't deemed it appropriate to read some composition of
his own, in order to cap off our little poetry reading, where, for the
first time, I saw poets face to face, in the exhibition of their work. It
was a dramatic poem destined for the Folies-Marigny. Distant
dream! Alas! We writhed on our seats. The blond Adelphe Froger
was rolling with laughter; the dark-haired Nodaret chuckled; me,
ever stern, but no longer impassive, I giggled. What verse! What literature!

I learned, while listening to those unspeakable things, that
certificates from the master of masters were simply a gesture of
well-wishing, and were inconsequential. That consoled me to be
without one.

After that rhapsody, whose length went well beyond all permissible limits, had finally been read, with his glass of sweetened
water half drunk, and the voice of the hoarse orator, the dark-haired
Nodaret exclaimed:

"Well! and that journal!"

Then, calmly, with the attitude of a proper notary, of an irreproachable lawyer, M. T*** recited a small discourse in which he demonstrated that with money one could work miracles, at first! Then, that *ten* literary hacks sufficed, young doubtless, but capable of giving one hundred francs per month, to make a poetic journal come alive. He requested by way of conclusion, given we were already *four* voters, that he be named the editor in chief, and allowed us to go, throughout the city, to find the other future shareholders.

That's how things work in Paris. M. T***, whose name I withhold, was able to believe that that was a fine job. I saw very respectable, reputable men make naïve fellows pay one franc, fifty centimes for each inserted verse. From that, almost banal, contestation (one knew so many similar agencies), I draw two conclusions: that poetry is so honored in this country that, to win the title of bard, many retired commandants, fatigued preceptors, lettuce merchants, or magistrates, greedy for gain for themselves or their next of kin, sometimes riddled with debts, do not hesitate spending their money in order to have themselves published. Poetry and vanity! It's on that second sin that they count, the entrepreneurs of small poetic journals, *edited by the subscribers*, so goes the prospectus! where unfortunate poets pay through the teeth for the glory of enriching the cuisine of two or three joyous skeptics who resell by weight the inevitable *bullion* of their journals. Poor suckers for the dream!

Fortunately, although quite naïve myself, I put my two young colleagues on guard against the industrialist in question.

And when that fantastical M. T*** had finished, we rapidly left, him, his drama, his sugar, his water, his spoon, his journal, and his chandeliers illuminating his little desert, which, even if it had been furnished with chairs like so many palm trees, was absolutely deprived of the various and sundry sources required by travelers lost in those thirsty climes.

All three of us, – the three poets!! – we descended, and, at the nearest café, we went on to discourse on the fate of modern poetry.

Edmond Nodaret was a lowly employee like me; only he aimed for direct contributions. Adelphe Froger, still a minor, was due, at his majority, to come into possession of a rather large sum of money: – o joy! - he was going to consecrate it to literature... and throw into poetry – o bottomless pit – the accumulated sweat of his forefathers.

He was a young man taken with art; his verse, which did not show an extreme originality, stood on its own well enough, better than many others', and a good judge in such matters, Catulle Mendès, did not hesitate to prove it to him by sharing with Froger the title of editor in chief of *The Republic of Letters*. They founded – *The Renaissanc*e being dead – a new review, serious that one, and truly artistic, the memory of which is not lost; for it accommodated *l'Assommoir* by Zola, a general outcast at that time. Nevertheless, it also died, not without resistance, but it did die.

The Bohemian life of young literary hacks is full of laughs, and songs, beneath which can be heard the profound *Dies iræ* of the *Nunc dimittis* of a bunch of dying journals. The story of poets is a necrology of leaves, and Millevoye was quite right when he said:

With the defoliation of our woods,
Autumn had strewn the earth with leaves.

Or also, the singer, saying:

Poor leaves, waltz, waltz! (bis.)

But through Froger, having become editor in chief, I was able finally to view up close, as much as possible for a myope, and to touch poets with my hands, no longer in the solemnity of café Tabourey or café Voltaire; but in a minuscule brasserie called the *Sherry-Cobbler*, which is worth several lines of memory.

That *Sherry-Cobbler*, situated on boulevard Saint-Michel – the center of affairs, o poetry! between Saint-Louis High School and Derenne Bookstore where *The République des Lettres* was produced, – was run by a stunningly beautiful blonde woman, Joséphine, who after many misadventures ended up relocating to Texas to establish a brasserie. One was served – served is a manner of speaking, you will see why – by the young and pretty girls, many of whom had chosen their path in life. But that which, from the very beginning, distinguished the *Sherry-Cobbler* from all other brasseries was that there was never any drink available called the *sherry-cobbler*, that American beverage being as profoundly unknown there as Homeric ambrosia was; none of the comers or goers can vaunt having, by the aid of a straw, wetted their whistle with that special nectar, which served however as the ensign of the modest establishment run by Joséphine.

One evening, three bold high-school students – that age is merciless – three high-school students, their mouths equipped with enormous panatellas, cigars like rhinoceros horns, entered into that place of lyricism and, o stupor, ordered from the young girl who waited on them:

"Three sherry-cobblers!"

Three sherry-cobblers, three! One sherry-cobbler would have been bold enough, but three! The prepossessed blond, not familiar with that beverage, immediately thought it was a bad joke on the part of those schoolboys; then, on their insistence, she took off to the cashier, and repeated the order on the part of the wild and extravagant clients:

"Tell them we are out," said the cashier, to save the honor of the flag.

It was at that paradoxical place where poets assembled, and where I came myself, finally delivered of my timidity, to sit in turn. I didn't dare however raise my voice in the literary cenacle; I listened, as was fitting for a good neophyte; I heard the bold assertions, the rude repartees, the marvelous dissertations, that shined, when Coppée, Mendès, Mérat, Paul Arène, Stéphane Mallarmé, Villiers de l'Isle-Adam, Valade, since passed away, that poet who signed adorable rhymed columns as Silvius and of whom Monselet said:

And I see a young Valade,
A young Valade with slow gait,

when so many poets, Parnassian or not, Baudelairean or Poesque, met with their cadets, Richepin, Bouchor, Bourget, Rollinat, A. Froger, Ponchon, the painter Tanzi, Michel de l'Hay, Guillaume Livet, the attorney Adrien Lefort, Alexandre Hepp, who had just published his first book of verse, Vautrey, Edmond Deschaumes, fresh out of middle school.

Here I cite several lines published in *The Voltaire* by Guillaume Livet:

> *There (at the Sherry) one talked a lot, one drank solidly, and one dreamt of the future.*

> *In the corner sat, from the hour of absinthe to the hour of closing, a tall, very dark-haired young man, with hair in his face and a pointed beard, like Mounet-Sully, remarkable by his face which had a Meridional character to it; he drank amply, without getting drunk, but he didn't say a word, listening instead, tranquilly, to the great artistic discussions, and making so little noise that one didn't pay attention to him, and looked upon him as if he were one of the pieces of furniture – to be ceded with the business on the day of bankruptcy.*

> *"Who is that gentleman?" someone asked one day.*

> *"It's Émile Goudeau, an employee of the ministry of finance," responded disdainfully the proprietress.*

> *And there were no more questions. A good comrade otherwise, he often accompanied us on our travels through Paris, and, ever solid, helped back to their lodging those among us who had been incommoded by beer.[9]*

Ah! yes! I savored the bizarre joy of rubbing elbows with the people who were published in the gazettes, nearly famous beings, at least from Bullier's to the Moulin de la Galette.[10] Otherwise, what good could come of my trying to put myself on the same footing as those Parisians, from the get-go? When I opened up to one of them,

---

[9]Original footnote: *The Voltaire*, Sunday, 3 December 1882.

[10]Bullier's... Moulin de la Galette: two dance halls, one covered, the other open. See also Paul Alexis' *La Fin de Lucie Pellegrin (Snuggly Books, 2020)*.

one evening, about my poetical projects, he exclaimed with a nuance of regret:

"So, you are no longer the good Gascon who does not write verse! Oh! you would like to resemble others? Fi! fi then!"

Thus did he speak to me, the poet Germain Nouveau, he who has since then become a painter. Nonetheless, that I might have a small part in future dreams, it was decided that I would be a dramatic author.

I took that vague role to heart, and began slaving away in silence on a comedy in verse.

The supernumerary! And a comedy in verse! From time to time, just barely, an uncle of mine would send me meager subsidies that, like roses, lasted the space of a morning; alas! a depressing anguish often grabbed hold of me in that furnished and sweating hotel; I didn't possess any easy laughter within those four solitary walls. So I hurried outside to inhale the fine gaiety of young poets and their camaraderie. The *illustrious Sapeck*, eccentric painter, with the cold and serious outward appearance of a splenetic Englishman, was the cheerer-upper in person, the life of the party. It was he who, seeing songs dozing in dry throats, cried out: "Let's get some champagne!"

And we clinked glasses, while singing:

In the garden of my fatherland
The lilacs are in bloom,
In the garden of my fatherland
The lilacs are in bloom;
All the birds on earth
Come to make their nests there;
Next to his blonde
It's so good, it's so good, it's so good,
Next to his blonde
It's so good to fall asleep.

Or even this other song, by Marguerite (or Madeleine), of which here's one version (there are many others):

Marguerite did her hair

With six bottles of wine,
        Marguerite did her hair
        With six bah – ah – ah,
        With six bah – ah – ah,
With six bottles of wine.

Marguerite, she feels ill,
She needs to see a doctor;
Marguerite, she feels ill,
        She nee – ee – ee,
        She nee – ee – ee ,
She needs to see a doctor.

On her first visit,
He forbade her the wine;
On her first visit,
        He forba – aa – aa,
        He forba – aa – aa,
He forbade her the wine.

Go to hell, Doctor,
Me, I love my wine too much;
Go to hell, Doctor,
        Me, I luh – uh – uh,
        Me, I luh – uh – uh,
Me, I love my wine too much.

If I die, bury me
In a cave where there is wine,
If I die, bury me
        In a cave where – there – is
        In a cave where – there – is
In a cave where there is wine.

Feet against the wall,
Her head under the faucet;
Feet against the wall,
        Her head und – er – the,
        Her head und – er – the,
Her head under the faucet.

If some drops should drip,
That would be to refresh;
If some drops should drip,
    That would be to – re,
    That would be to – re,
That would be to refresh.

If the cask were staved in,
I'd drink to my heart's content;
If the cask were staved in,
    I'd drink – to – my,
    I'd drink – to – my,
I'd drink to my heart's content.

Once the gaiety had started up, there was no stopping it, and the poets, standing on the tables, declaimed their verse with great and crazy gestures, making their brown or blond hair jump up, verse still hot off the recent anvil, and which didn't cool down by publication in book form.

For, despite that cabaret life, one worked hard, nobody knew where or when; nonetheless the poems accumulated piece by piece, through the disjointedness of existence.

In the evening, late, while going home, the poets pointed out with their finger the Odeon, the promised land. One evening even, under the arcades, three among them swore eternal loyalty to each other, reciprocal aid, so as to conquer glory. They called themselves, out of hatred for the dying past, which it seemed, was going to disappear before their nascent dawn, *The Living.* Quite full of life, they were, in effect, Jean Richepin, Paul Bourget, and Maurice Bouchor.

Destiny did not fail them in the least.

Chapter Three

Maurice Bouchor: Joyous Songs. – *Jean Richepin:* The Beggars' Song. –
The Turco-Greek Restaurant. – Paul Bourget: The Troubled Life, Edel. –
The Haitians, Raoul Ponchon, and the illustrious Sapeck.

Maurice Bouchor had just published with Charpentier his first volume of verse, *Joyous Songs.*[11] The critics received it with a salvo of
praise, that work of an eighteen-year-old poet, who, cavalierly, entered, with a smile on his lips, into the ancient domain of poetry.

"Ah! that domain, how serious one has made it: a sort of
huge temple of worship, but deserted, where the rare faithful speak
in hushed tones of voice. Alas! Alas! a theory of choirboys raised in
the fateful shadow of that sanctuary, dark in spite of their blond and
curly hair, gave off a faint odor of old cathedrals, exotic pagodas,
German consistories, Biblical candles, and old frocks: some obscure
and salt-petered chapel's effluvium."

So thought the Revolutionary Maurice Bouchor at that time;
he pitted the simplicity of his manner against alembicated and con-
voluted procedures, and his love for fresh air against the fragrances
of closed, stuffy rooms.

With the audacity of a student who *skips* school and *plays
hooky*, he flouted the indoctrinating masters in cathedra, and ran towards the lively street, to cast his impressions on passersby, as when
during the carnival in Nice people hit each other with flowers.

"Let's forget them," he seemed to say to his comrades, "let's
forget those professors of poetic horticulture, who take roses in order
to package them symmetrically and lay them, in too-tightly bound
bouquets, on solemn cenotaphs! Let's forget the botanizing person-
ages who cull fresh and living violets, at the far side of embank-
ments in the woods, to catalog them in an herbarium. Let's forget the
collectors of butterflies who think they are sages by contemplating
the prodigious colors that the thin cadavers conserve while pinned.
Let's forget the bird catchers of syllables, who imprison rhymes be-

---

[11] *Joyous Songs: les Chansons joyeuses.*

hind rules of iron wire! Better to prefer – to all those poems of distant isles, to all the cockatoos, the macaws, the cardinals, and other rare fowls that one shows off with pride in an aviary that is duly enclosed, – the simple crows of the Luxembourg Gardens, and the chaffinches of the *jardin des Plantes*, and the common sparrows of the squares."

So, passing nimble and disdainful before the flower bouquet chapel, and the bird-catcher hotel de Rambouillet, he rejoiced in the lively street, and gave *joyous songs* to those who wished to hear them.

He particularly repudiated that expression of a polisher of rhymes:

And we make touching rhymes very emotionlessly.

He became emotional himself for no reason, on the contrary, and without fake Dandyism sang his impressions like others in the same period, trying to depict them on canvas.

More than one of those young songs has remained in the memory of those who heard them. Here's one, chosen at random:

The notary will dress in black...
Those people, it's so morose!
You, you will dress in white and pink,
Having, for so grave a thing,
Consulted with your mirror.

And then, with a smile on our lips,
With light feet, and open hearts,
In the sunlight, near green meadows.
We will betake ourselves
To the smiling hillocks of Sèvres.

All alone, singing and blessed!
At our feet, ripe strawberries!
In our faces, the long murmurs
That are heard in the boughs
Where nests are hidden.

And the dead, under the thick grass –
If, by hazard, we pass
Close to a cemetery – to the sounds
Of our joyous songs,
Will dream of their youth.

And the skies will be set
On your head and on mine,
And, down there, in the plain
O pretty one, I will lead you,
To hunt for kisses.

Not long afterwards, *Songs of Love and the Sea* appeared. The poet seemed to have grown melancholic in it. The critics were surprised and made the young poet pay somewhat for the success of his first work. One of the harshest pannings came precisely from *The Republic of Letters*; it's appropriate to add that, in a note placed at the top of the article where Maurice Bouchor was rather roughly treated, the editorial staff cleared itself of any responsibility.

He was reproached for the banality of his subject, which, by parenthesis, is quite extraordinary, given that that was his design, and that it is precisely love of the eminent, the unknown, or the un-recognizable that renders poetry abstruse, indecipherable. Only a sincere poet knows how to make banality itself poetic.

"After having declared," exclaimed the article's author, "that he hated all things old, M. Maurice Bouchor falls into the same trap and uses the same procedures. His volume may be a journal of his heart, but it's not a work... We say nothing about the prosodic licenses that M. Jean Richepin's friend takes affectatiously. It's a system."

M. de Banville, in an article on *The Songs of Love and the Sea*, wrote more kindly:

"... To be sure, what we have here is great, sane, and robust poetry. My heart of an old Romantic goes out quite a bit when I see AMOUR in remarkable rhyming with VELOURS, and TRÈVE without "s" rhyming with SOULÈVES; but why not! I'm OLD SCHOOL. These young fellows have raised the banner of revolt; they have victoriously pulled down and broken my old idol, and what was an EXACT RHYME has become a goddess without arms, like the Venus de Milo!"

Well said!

In order to get some rest, doubtless, and to get the better of Victor Hugo himself, Maurice Bouchor left Paris to settle down on Guernsey, in the company of Jean Richepin and his faithful companion Raoul Ponchon. He dated, from that famous isle, his poems and sent them to *The Republic of Letters*, which inserted them out of respect for the postal stamp: Guernsey!

That wasn't at all, however, a place of perfect deliciousness, that rock, from what I can tell by certain epistles, which the *illustrious Sapeck* ought still to possess. They complained bitterly about the absence of a ton of things, above all the absence of Paris and Parisians. Sapeck, being unable to send them what they asked for, counseled them to return from exile. So they did.

Maurice Bouchor had set out to be a fantasist Bohemian by predilection, and not by force, like so many others, including Richepin, the *king of beggars*. Bouchor, the red-haired Creole, with the Anglo-Saxon features, a strong drinker, with reddish complexion, was from then on wealthy and didn't much resemble the pale poets who wear down the fresh flower of their young gaiety against poverty.

Among his comrades, he was first to be published, while Richepin lugged around here and there his *Beggars' Song*, Paul Bourget his *Troubled Life*, Maurice Rollinat his *Poem of the Heaths*.

It was strange! He became nevertheless the most splenetic among them. His *Joyous Songs* didn't take long to turn into melancholic sonnets, into sad tales. With each passing year, he grew more distant from his friends-in-arms of the first hour; he began to adore music and even mathematics. At this very moment that I'm writing, he has perhaps plunged into *differential Calculus*.[12]

At that time, Jean Richepin alluding doubtless to some deep,

---

[12]Original footnote: those musical and mathematical studies were the preparation for a synthesis. Maurice Bouchor, in his *Symbols*, his latest book, presented, like a magician, ancient and modern rites under the sacred habit of poetic rhymes.

and possibly incurable, love, addressed this sonnet to him:

> *Let your mistress be blonde, auburn, or brunette,*
> *Let her come from on high, below, or elsewhere,*
> *Fear certain abandonment as promised by mockers.*
> *Woman and her desires are regulated by the moon.*
>
> *All love in the world has a common end.*
> *Your mistress will take your best years,*
> *And she'll despoil them under her wasteful fingers.*
> *Woman is a danger, when one loves only one.*
>
> *Love them all, then: that's the surest bet;*
> *The brunette with night eyes, the blonde with azure eyes.*
> *The auburn with sea eyes, and many others still.*
>
> *Do not fix your heart on their deceiving hearts!*
> *But change! The happy man is he who dons*
> *The hat of lovers, which turns with each blowing wind.*

To which Bouchor simply responded: "I'm monogamous!"

Richepin, meanwhile, found a publisher, Maurice Dreyfous. I can still hear the lovely literary racket that that superb volume of poetry stirred up: *Beggars' Song*.[13]

For those who still remembered the glow of fires burning during the Commune, that *Song*, having rapidly become the song of the *Coq rouge*,[14] which would have quickly re-awoken from within the tangled bushes, on the ruins of the Tuileries and the palace of the Court of Revenue.

> *Open the door*
> *To the little ones who are cold.*
> *The little ones clack their teeth.*
> *Ohé! They hear you!*

---

[13] *Beggars' Song: la Chanson des gueux.*

[14] *Coq rouge*: Red Cock, a symbol of revolution, of revolutionary spirit, from the Commune particularly in this case. Like a Phoenix rising up from its ashes, the people rise up from their persecutions...

If it's warm there inside,
        Good people,
It's quite cold on the street.

        Open the door
To the little ones who are hungry.
The little ones clack their teeth
Ohé! They must come in!
You eat there inside,
        Good people, –
They've nothing in their belly.

        Open the door
To the little ones who are tired.
The littles clack their teeth.
Ohé! They need the barn!
You sleep there inside,
        Good people,
Their eyes, they irritate you.

        Open the door
For the little ones with a lighter
The little ones gnash their teeth.
Ohé! They're hard of hearing!
We will see there inside,
        Good people,
If the fire should wake you.

The epithet chosen by Maurice Bouchor to characterize this highly colorful poetry – the *living*, – does not seem to cut it; Jean Richepin invented the term *brutalism*: to capture, no longer just the life in poetry, but the violence. Instead of the gently modulated song of the last choir boys who accompanied the Romantic mass, cries from the public place, disorderly refrains from the horde of beggars: beggars from the fields, beggars from the highways, beggars from the cities and tenements (more or less furnished), working-class beggars and poetic beggars.

Come to me, feet-draggers,
Raggedy people, accordionists,
Laggers, good-for-nothings, hooligans, sluts,
And pip-squeaks and street urchins.

Pile of ass-dragging boots,
Race of fiery independenters!
I'm of your same country:
The poet is the King of Beggars.

Leaving the bourgeois clan behind for pure Bohemianism, the poet Jean Richepin consecrated himself the King of Panhandlers. He then went on to fasten, like a distinctive mark of that strange dignity, a good-luck bracelet onto his left wrist; for crown, he donned a hat of special shape. There was even, between the poor and great caricaturist André Gill and Jean Richepin, an epic battle, a peaceful quarrel to see who would unearth, from among the divers hatters of Paris, the bizarrest head-covering. Sometimes Gill had the advantage; but often Richepin came out ahead. The illustrator Sapeck would be the judge and would offer the palm to the winner.

Jean Richepin was not at all then a funereal poet. The philosophy of his brutalist beggars did not always appear as fierce as that of the *little ones* armed with a lighter. No. They are more mocking than anything, setting an example of good humor: like someone who sings, while watching the peasants breaking their back at work.

Who's a beggar?
Is it us,
Or rather those with
Two cents to rub together?
What a job for a large orchestra!
They're not someone to envy.
That goes from the first of January
To the Eve of Saint-Sylvestre.[15]

That wily spectator concludes:

---

[15]Eve of Saint-Silvestre: New Year's Eve.

Go, go, into the earth
Sling yer wheat! But what rotten luck!
Need t'cut me my crust
From yer proprietor's bread.
    Who's a beggar?
    Is it us,
    Or rather those with
    Two cents to rub together.

Above all, in the piece entitled *Migratory Birds,*[16] the sheer disdain that beggars profess, free and proud of their cares, in respect to farmyard poultry, whose boringly happy life is not designed to seduce the adventuresome migratory birds, is on display.

That turkey has always blessed his fate.
And, when the time comes to die, one must see
That young goose in tears: "This is where I was born,
I die near my mother and I have done my duty."

Only, society, represented by the judges of the correctional police, avenges itself cruelly on the poet: a month of prison for an attack on public mores, loss of political and civil rights, etc. Ah! You are the king of beggars, wait! You will never, never in your life, be a municipal councillor.

The poet of beggars spends his month in prison at Sainte-Pélagie. On the evening of his release, enthusiastic students carried him triumphantly to the Bal Bullier.[17] André Gill, who, himself, had never been carried in triumph, contented himself by declaiming in that inimitable accent of his, in which nobody could figure out whether the illustrator was mocking the audience or speaking seriously when he said: "Me! if I entered Paris on a white horse one would name me emperor!"

Beggars' Song had been prosecuted and condemned for two or three pieces, in which the poet tackled head on certain realities that are spoken about, every day, in divers news items and the col-

---

[16]*Migratory Birds: les Oiseaux de passage.*

[17]Bal Bullier: The Bullier Ballroom or dance hall.

umns of a multitude of journals.

But, shh! The theme will not be mentioned here; in this case, I follow Jean Richepin's advice instead: in the preface of the latest edition, he writes this:

"As for what relates to justice, you will allow me (dear reader) to imitate the good soldier who, according to M. Scribe, must suffer to keep quiet without murmuring."

Only, he rebelled with good reason against the hardly confraternal act of the journal that had denounced him on the parquet. That journal, it was – would you believe it? – the *Charivari*. In the name of what esthetic, of what moral laws, of what particular religion, of what divinity, or of what pagoda, did that unexpected preacher fulminate anathema against a poet? It's a mystery.

One of the most bizarre criticisms that was addressed at Richepin was his having punctuated his verse with apostrophes, as in the following:

Avoir l'air d'un mâl' v'là c'que j'gobe.[18]

Thin argument! He made his characters speak just as he had heard them sing, with the hiatuses and slang. Some beggars don't know orthography; and, in that complex book, each must have his place.

In revenge, listen to how Jean Richepin changes tone when he addresses himself to the poet, king of luminous spaces:

Let your hair be the tail end
Of a comet, and royally
Expose your blue banner to the wind,
Cut against the firmament.

Climb higher, like an eagle,
Ever higher, like a condor;
Climb unbridled, lawless, ruleless,
And lose yourself in the setting gold.

---

[18]*Avoir... j'gobe*: To have the air of a male, behold what I swallow.

And drift finally with full sales.
Far from the world, far from here;
Let your tears be stars,
And your perspirations oceans.

And up there, in the free space,
On your glorious and handsome body,
If you find there remains a trace
Of the struggle or of the stage,

On your face, if you see still
Some mud and bright blood,
Wash your face in the dawn
And dry yourself in the sun.

In order to dry himself in the sun, he deserted the *Sherry-Cobbler* on occasion for the Orient. The Orient, with a gracefulness that only he could savor, feeling himself too distant from Parisian poets, too distant, over there, near Asia Minor and the archipelagoes, he took off for rue Monsieur-le-Prince, specifically for a Turco-Greek restaurant. We joined him and went there to lunch on shish kebab, to eat bizarre cakes and confitures of roses imported from Smyrna; we drank raki and zwicka there. There were two patrons, the one serious, serving Turkish coffee with an Ottoman majesty, the other active and petulant, always carrying hidden up his long sleeve a sharp stiletto that we called the Palikar's khanjar. Ohé! King of the mountains!

It's from there that, one evening, a young Walachian, who sometimes composed verse, departed. His suicide was perpetrated in an extremely dignified fashion, with a perfect Dandyism. D***, dressed in new clothes, bouquets in hand, presented himself at the till and, graciously, decorated the counter, and cashier's corsage, with flowers. Then, addressing himself to a student of medicine, he said to him, nonchalantly:

"My dear friend, I wager that the small tip of the heart is found here between these two ribs." And he designated a point beneath his tight waistcoat.

"Not at all," retorted the other, "it's lower. There!"

"I lose then," responded D***, satisfied...

He called for a fiacre, which arrived, and he gave the command that he be conducted to the Arc de Triomphe.

When the coachman, having arrived at the end of the Champs -Élysées, opened the door, he found only a cadaver on the cushions. D*** had shot himself in the heart with a revolver.

As they were taking him away, a young woman, who had gotten down from her coupé, remarked that the ankle boots of the deceased had not been worn; there was not a speck of dust on their yellow soles.

People, correct or not, are not always happy people.

"Another glass of racki, monsieur the patron."

One found Paul Bourget there, he who rarely came to the Sherry-Cobbler, to take part in the poetic tumultuousness that our exuberant youth gave itself over to. Bourget had little passion of life for life itself, at that time; he conceived of life only literarily; he was, above all, an artist. Here's how he spoke:

Days will follow each other, and the years,
Will lose their leaves like withered roses,
Before I hold in these feeble arms
The only treasures I have worshipped on earth:
Glory and genius. And, yet, how I love
These Letters that I make my supreme voluptuousness!
How I feel my entire heart vibrate with these words!
The pleasures and troubles they've lavished on me,
The impassioned nights I have consumed
To espy a phrase in flight, and the days!
Yes, even when April smiled in a clear sky,
Even when a flower's scent floated in the air
Suave and delicate like a woman's breath,
I locked myself in, closing my eyes, mastering my soul,
Drunk with my work and ready to kill myself
To vanquish finally the rebellious word, and create.

To create! to feel the words twitching on the page,
To hear them shiver with love, and hurl with rage,
And myself with them, vibrating, suffering, crying.
To be with them like God in the world, to create!

That little resembled the theories of the Living and the Brutalists; but what greatly endeared the poet to his friends was the
predilection he had in any case for what has since then been called
modernism, that is to say, with the exclusion of ancient legends and
tales from the Middle Ages, research into the present moment, into
the hour that passes with us, and which sings or weeps in our smiles
or our tears, as living beings.

Paul Bourget believed in solitary labor, in the cenobitism of
the thinker, the analyst, and the bibliophile. Great admirer, profound
devotee of Balzac, he waved the banner of Balzacians amidst the
Living and the Brutalists. His Balzacianism went very far. In his
modest, but very correct, apartment on rue Guy-de-la-Brosse, from
which one could see the trees in the *jardin des Plantes* blossoming
little by little over the course of beautiful mornings in April, and towards autumn displaying themselves in multicolor splashes through
his windows, Paul Bourget submitted himself to a strict Balzacian
regime: dining very early, going to bed soon thereafter, then waking
before the crack of dawn, at three in the morning, as he wrote in his
poem *Edel*:

One, two, three. Yes, it's three o'clock. In the night,
How plaintive it is, that cry of the hour that runs away!
To better hear it ringing, I have put down my quill,
And behold how with that fateful sound a fog
Of dolorous dreams envelopes me, and I hear
Pass over me the terrifying breath of time.

The reclusive poet knocked back two or three bowls of black
coffee, like Balzac, and, like Balzac, worked until seven in the morning. Then he went back to sleep for one hour, before waking definitively, and going out to ply the mean but lucrative occupations that
the poverty of beginnings imposes on young literary hacks. All day
long then, Paul Bourget, no longer Balzacian, but a licentiate of letters, taught Latin and Greek to aspirants to the baccalaureate; he

poured into rebellious skulls the entirety of antiquity, and coming away, doubtless, from this Danaïde profession, with a certain disgust for antiquity, refreshed himself in the evening in full modernism.

But, alas! in the society of young companions, he quickly found himself tired, falling asleep for fatigue, and no longer able to live but on the express condition of going to bed at eight o'clock in the evening to rise at three in the morning. The sheets of blank paper, placed in piles on the work table, called him at the back of rue Guy-de-la-Brosse; at the end of a meal, at the moment when the Turco-Greek mocha was steaming in his cup, the large bowl full of cold coffee, destined to wake him up again at three in the morning, seemed to be saying to him: "Come with us! Leave these people then who exhaust the dear present moment in sterile discussions, fleeting eloquence, future diagnostics and prognostics; come with us, repose beside us, then rise before dawn! Drink me, said the mocha! Cover us with your chicken scratch, the sheets of blank paper sang!"

Soon, however, he realized on his own that to frequent exclusively Balzac, Byron, Heinrich Heine, and Stendhal, he would grow anemic. His comrades said to him: "He will become like Sainte-Beuve, the great critic of our generation." That displeased the poet of *The Troubled Life*.[19]

Certainly the *The Lively Life*[20] attracted not a few imitators as well; he wrote in the preface to the poem *Edel*, which he composed at that time and which Lemerre published (1878), that very significative program:

"And here we are forty years since the most astonishing genius of the nineteenth century, everyone's father, the great Balzac, magisterially put forward the modern ideal: 'With every generation,' he said, 'there is a drama played out by four or five thousand individuals that literature has the duty to express,' under pain of becoming what was, in Rome at the time of Claudian,[21] a sterile arrangement of dead syllables. That principle has brought the art of writing back to a lively psychology, and has renewed criticism and the nov-

---

[19] *The Troubled Life: la Vie inquiète.*

[20] *The Lively Life: la Vie vivante.*

[21] Claudian: Claudius Claudianus (AD 384-423), a Latin poet during the reign of Roman Emperor Honorius.

el, just as it has renewed history. Does it bring with it a new poetry, destined to occupy a brilliant place between the historical poetry so marvelously represented by Leconte de Lisle, and Romantic poetry whose followers of Hugo carry the old flag with valiancy? For my part, I believe it with all sincerity of conscience. I see clearly what needs to be done so that poetry might be created. Alas! it is enough for me to re-read *Edel* in order to notice once again that, in literature as in life, man realizes his dreams with difficulty."

To be noted in these lines are the proclamation of Balzac's superiority over Hugo, the allusion to Claudian, and the pronounced tendency towards psychological analysis.

Only, the brutal ways of life on the roads and highways, the atmosphere of the street, the seedy dives, the proclivities for noctambulism, the little Bohemian's celebrations, repugned him:

> *I sat down in the isolated corner of a café;*
> *I saw in the thick and over-heated atmosphere,*
> *Hunched over their glass where the absinthe turned white,*
> *Thirty-year-old men who, with pupils faded,*
> *And already bald, smoked while reading a journal.*
> *The sound of their voices grew louder. A trivial people*
> *Of tired brokers, gloomy journalists,*
> *And extremely young men already weary and sad,*
> *Huddled under the gas flames that mixed*
> *Lugubriously with the pale light of day that was ending.*
> *I sat with my elbows for a long time on the marble table,*
> *Nearly in tears, drowned in ineffable grief:*
> *For that was, that dolorous café, after leaving*
> *The palace wherein my heart had felt so much,*
> *The symbol, visible to me alone, of the life*
> *That would seize me one day when my soul, ravished*
> *Into a blue paradise of supernatural love,*
> *Would fall flat again onto the real world.*

> *– Edel*

I cite these lines of verse, not because they are the best that Bourget has ever written, but to indicate the state of soul in which he found himself at that time, the immense need he felt to escape from *that real world* composed of Bohemians and the Villons of pubs, in order to escape towards that aristocratic, delicate, and quintessential sphere, in which he needed to isolate himself much later.

The field of *modern life* is very vast; there are rooms whose lights, in the evening, respond to the twinkling gas lamps of the grogshop; and princess Morphine is as real as Coupeau.[22] Paul Bourget would prefer the princess already, and his psychological analysis needed to concentrate more on the refined nuances of the world than the brutal colors of the crowd.

> *Oh! the rabble, those whose bitter jobs,*
> *Like an indefatigable iron hammer, pound*
> *The human animal day and night and murder it!*
> *It seems to me that while trucking my spirit there,*
> *By rubbing elbows with the downtrodden and subjugated*
> *   [masses,*
>
> *My desire will be reborn to writhe this life,*
> *To wring from it whatever beauty it contains.*
> *Let me pull myself together for the modernness*
> *Of a fury that my entire soul is filled with.*
>
> *...................................... On every horizon,*
> *Nothing but a mass of sweating black tenements*
> *And, from one place to another, a window,*
> *Lit up and hiding some drama maybe,*
> *A sinister eye, marked by a blood spot.*
> *The omnibuses ran everywhere, splattering mud*
> *On the masses, tossing about on the pavement, enormous,*
> *Filthy, stinking, like deformed monsters.,*
> *And the gas lights, palpitant breath, blazed...*

My how one senses that the poet adores the padded lounge, wall hangings, chandeliers, a large grand piano, partitions here and there, an emblazoned wall clock, thick rugs, a fireplace that one leans against in order to recite poetry.

---

[22]Coupeau; a character in the novel, *l'Assommoir*, by Zola, who starts out sober enough, but ends up a flat out drunk and ultimately raving mad.

It is not by *snobbism*, but by the deep predilection for a special modernity that the poet of *Edel* becomes a *dandy*. His penetrating analysis needs the study of more complicated, more alembicated, more contoured souls than those of naïve people who expose their passions to the sun, like Venus who, shamelessly, shows off her torso; he wants to overcome the difficulty of penetrating through the fabric, the doublet, the corsage, and the false collar to get at the heart. Already, he is researching *Enigmas*. A modern Œdipus, he advances on the worldly steppes and mirages in order to interrogate the *Sphinxes* that appear all the more ambiguous in their responses, as they often have nothing to say, as it so happens.

Like a professor of dandyism, Paul Bourget had the happy fortune of finding a master in M. Barbey d'Aurevilly. Here's the portrait that the young poet draws of the old fighter:

> .... *The old master*
> *To begin with, Jean d'Altaï, the terrible, that roughneck*
> > *[soldier*
> *Of the serialized novel, for whom the quill is a knife:*
> *A caged eagle using its beak against the bars.*
> *Handlebar mustache, lace on his tie,*
> *A scarlet stripe on his white pair of trousers,*
> *Rhinegrave pinched at the waist, he has the look*
> *Of a pirate-dandy who's about to go to sea;*
> *That man writes, like he dresses: he is bizarre*
> *But exquisite, violent but strong, sought-after but rare.*

From that moment forward, Paul Bourget snubbed the blank pages and bowls of coffee at three in the morning. He went with Jean d'Altaï, on circus Saturdays, he ventured out in blue-green pants, unusual ties. His deep-set taste for society life saved him quickly, fortunately, from any eccentric genre.

He remained a good comrade, the best perhaps, the quickest to render a service. Sunday mornings, in his small room on rue Guy-de-la-Brosse, he fraternally received young comrades, who sometimes tarried there until the hour of lunch, often just after.

Richepin stayed there two weeks even, and, because he wanted to use his only suit of clothes sparingly, he went about the apartment and received visitors, dressed simply in a kind of ridiculous dressing gown cut from an old curtain.

But the poet of *Beggars* had soon succeeded in scraping together enough money, and resumed his bizarre lifestyle, with improbable hats on his head, rings on his fingers, bracelets on his wrists – what am I saying? gold rings clasped around his ankle. He was followed about by an anonymous and vague crowd, in which one could make out in particular Haitian negroes – a boisterous cortege – the *negues*, for whom the "r" didn't exist any more than it did for the old *Incoyables*.[23] Among this group of dark individuals, Ponchon gleamed, and Sapeck, the illustrious Sapeck, would stand out pale; Ponchon sang about wine, and Sapeck drew, with a swift pencil, his caricatures. They were famous in the Latin Quarter, and their names were frequently bound together.

There was however a great difference between those two figures. The illustrious Sapeck, tall, thin, simian-like in face, made for himself an original role as a *fumist*, after the example of Romieu and the Vivier horn. He possessed an English sportsman's elegance, and brought flowers to young people whom he honored with his favors. When the *Sherry-Cobbler*, presided over by Joséphine, found itself short on beverages, and couldn't satisfy the thirst of poets and dandies, Sapeck stepped up, correctly attired, roses in his buttonhole, then, discretely, stepped out to visit the neighboring grocer, to acquire, for some pretty pennies, some *reparative* vermouth, inspiring absinthe, consoling champagne, which, poured into glasses, and from there into brains, produced the tintinnabulating sonnets, marvelous ballads, and triolets of his friends the poets, Sapeck asked them for nothing in return but to preserve for him their manuscripts, the which, bound in a rich fashion, must have decorated his library.

Sapeck had, among other specialities, the gift of imitating ravishingly the cry of a pup *whose paw had been stepped on*. Now, he had a minuscule bow-wow by the name Tenny that he carried in the pocket of his enormous putty-colored *overcoat*. Sapeck lived, at that time, right in the heart of Montrouge; he was devoted to that distant quarter, being a pupil of André Gill, who claimed that the Mont-

[23]*incoyables*: A reference to the *Incroyables,* a short-lived group of upper class individuals during the French Revolution.

parnasse cemetery was at the *center of affairs*. Only, Sapeck often came down to place Saint-Michel. Wealthy, but thrifty, he took the tramway; however, he brought with him in the pocket of his coat, the young beast-dog, called *Tenny*. One evening, a grumpy conductor caught sight of Tenny's paw which was sticking out of the overcoat, and declared:

"Dogs don't ride the tramway."

The illustrious Sapeck did not allow himself to be disconcerted for such a little thing and, saluting the conductor, descended; then, seeing that bureaucrat occupied with collecting his fares, hailed an empty fiacre that was passing by, put his dog Tenny on the cushions, and, closing the door, asked the coachman to follow the tramway. After which, joyous, he remounted the platform of the tramway.

The conductor, at the moment that the illustrious Sapeck held out his six sous, recognized him for the man with the dog, and declared peremptorily that, having a dog in pocket, he could not participate in the honor, accorded to humans, of riding on the *Company General of Tramways*, it being expressly forbidden that said humans be accompanied by any animal.

The illustrious Sapeck swore to *the great gods* that he had no dog with him. At the next station, the tramway stopped. Discussion. The controller asks where the dog is that the conductor claims to have seen. The controversy didn't end there. The riders on the upper deck, less informed than those of the interior, stand up and lean over the balustrade, asking: "Is it broke down?"

The controller, against the exasperated conductor's advice, in the presence of Sapeck, who pretends to get undressed in order to show that he has absolutely no dog with him, makes the car move on.

The fiacre follows.

As soon as the illustrious Sapeck sits down on an empty seat and, abusing the gift that I spoke about earlier, a gift that consisted in imitating the cry of a dog *whose paw had been stepped on*, lets out a plaintive bark. The conductor jumps.

"I knew it!" he said with a triumphant air.

At the next station, the conductor and the controller explain:

"Monsieur, you have a dog, you must get off!"

The illustrious Sapeck proposes again to get undressed. Everyone on the interior of the bus laughs. The upper deck groans; the convulsed people lean over, demand what is happening, why has this ridiculous tramway stopped. The conductor exclaims:

"Not only did I see the dog, I heard it!..."

Sapeck dismounts then, and, to the acclamations of the multitude, goes to pick up *Tenny-Tenny* from the fiacre that was passively following the tramway all this time.

Such was Sapeck.

Raoul Ponchon was something else altogether. Having mounted the poetic tramway, he did not imitate any cry of a dog, nor that of Victor Hugo, Boileau, nor Stéphane Mallarmé. With an absolute independence, he dragged his life around wherever it pleased him. "Will he publish a volume," someone asked, "or won't he?" Idle question. He inspired, some said, modernist verse, but he disdained submitting to editorial exigencies. He sovereignly judged the merit of people, covered or bound, and for a long time remained content with that attitude.

But one could read some of his verse; *The Republic of Letters* published them. *The Riding Crop* (was it the *Riding Crop*?) published, around 1877, a satire wherein one reads, *that after all nothing surprises,* because

Adelphe Froger is someone, and Nodaret something.

Let's recall here that Adelphe Froger was the editor in chief of *The Republic of Letters* and that Nodaret signed the articles that targeted Richepin or Maurice Bouchor.

Here is some verse by Raoul Ponchon:

Hurrah! here's autumn,
Wine steams and bubbles;

Already I talk nonsense.

We're going, my friends,
To drink, alas! I shiver,
As if it's not permitted.

Already I'm prey
To the finest joy
And my dear nose shines.

Let's drink, eat, dance.
Loves, blonde cupbearers,
Pour us some songs.

Let's take those strong women:
– I call them our mistresses! –
There, let's untie their tresses;

And we'll sleep with them
In the vineyard, and we'll put
Rubies on their foreheads.

– Dance, my spider,
My mouth looks like it's bleeding,
Soaked in wine.

Wine, you bring counsel.
I drink your vermilion son
To your health, Sun!

And to yours, cutie,
Whose nose shines vermilion
And who is so good!

And to yours, sirs!
O delicious wine
From the caves of the sky,

Go, run, circulate, flow

In me, my head spins
Like a simple ball.

The god! here's the god!
I cannot take anymore: hey! hey!
Let's drink some more.

I'm a poor drunk!
That last drop, my ruddy face,
Will be for Poland!

And then, this postscriptum
For my nose, a geranium
Worthy of a museum.

You paint me rose skies
Like rose roses,
Rosé wine that moistens me.

I can no longer distinguish,
Jesus Christ from Bacchus,
The Virgin from Venus,

Day from night, one
From the other, blonde or brown
And my... from the moon.

(Republic of Letters, December 3, 1876.)

I added the ellipsis points; the reader can fill them in for himself. Another poem by Ponchon in the February 18, 1877 edition of *The Republic*. Some stanzas:

RENEWAL

O you whose lips are sealed!
Behold the months you love,
Magic months when apple trees
Cause pink stars to rain.

And the sentimental end, which is charming:

> *If I'm filled with a sweet emotion,*
> *It's for you, o my chatelaine,*
> *And it is your sweet breath:*
> *I smell a perfume beside me.*
>
> *It's you, you who make me live,*
> *And joy swells my flesh;*
> *It's your soul scattered in the air*
> *That I inhale and that intoxicates me.*

In those days, the poet Raoul Ponchon had no place to live. A strange and invertebrate *maître d'hôtel*, very unlike the Hospitaliers, showed him the door. What did Ponchon do? He wandered the streets, sad and monologuing. But one evening when he had had the joy of taking several morsels of sugar from a café, he gathered together an improbable number of famished and stray dogs. He led them, half begging, half threatening them, to the furnished hotel from which he had been expelled. He rang the bell with a violence; then he made the ferocious pooches enter, one by one, like *The Raft of the Medusa*[24] pooches, into the corridor, towards the stairway. It was two in the morning. Raoul Ponchon closed the door behind them; he heard indistinct barking from all the floors. He ran away, rapidly; he never discovered how it all turned out.

A remarkable period for the poet Raoul! He wore a Breton costume and slept in the restroom! Does he remember those days now that he's become the applauded and poetic "leader" of the *French Courrier*?

---

[24]The Raft of the Medusa: a painting (ca. AD 1819) by French artist Théodore Géricault, depicting a scene of a dozen or so half-starved, dying, or dead men on a small raft adrift at sea.

Chapter Four

Émile Zola, l'Assommoir, *and the deputy public prosecutor. – A reading at Mounet-Sully's. – The compatriot Saint-Germain. – Brasserie Racine. – Cabanel's model. – Georges Lorin and Maurice Rollinat. – The scene of a drama. – The game the* Greeks. *– A mended diplomatic affair.*

The Republic of Letters published Émile Zola's *l'Assommoir.* I had had, at long last, a sonnet inserted in that review; but I had the satisfaction of going nearly every week to correct the proofs at Meaux, at the printer Cognet's shop. It was always a matter of participating, in one fashion or another, at the making of the only literary journal that existed at the time.

As for *l'Assommoir,* a small adventure happened in that subprefecture of Seine-et-Marne, which shows how much more spiritual Émile Zola is than what one wants to grant him. I'm told it is authentic, and, in any case, it seems highly probable. The deputy public prosecutor was disturbed by certain passages in the novel, and he thought he had to summon either Catulle Mendès or Adelphe Froger, perhaps both, to inform them that he was going to start legal proceedings. Upon which, he was entreated to wait until Émile Zola, the principal party, was made aware. Which was done. Zola presented himself at the public prosecutor's office in Meaux, and defended his novel: "On the surface, it seemed to contain a prejudice for violence, but there was nothing at all of that; it was an artist's work, a work published in an artistic review, addressed only to readers taken with art, and quite above any such scandal; besides, the conclusion of the work, essentially moral, would show clearly what the author was trying to get at, who boasted of being a Frank, an honest bourgeois, etc., etc."

Zola has used the same arguments many a time since then; they were new at the time, and the deputy public prosecutor agreed not to bring the terrible powers of the law down on him – they were very severe at that time.

When the work came out in book form by the publisher

Charpentier, it was the public prosecutor's office of the Seine that was disturbed; but then – oh! then – he was told that what was able to be published without harm in Meaux, a provincial town, on 50-centime sheets, could not suddenly become harmful in Paris, the city of lights, in an edition for 3 fr. 50. It was in this way that *l'Assommoir* passed through mesh of justice's net.

The correcting of proofs was not sufficient for my young ambition; and, since I could not find a home for my verse in the anthologies, I resolved to follow the counsel of my comrades and try my hand at theater. O martyrology! grotesque martyrology!

Being a Perigordian, like Mounet-Sully, I addressed myself to the great tragedian whose star was starting to shine between court and garden, before the French public. He was living at that time on quai de Gesvres, on the fifth or sixth floor. There, I brought to him, one day, a copy of my comedy in modern verse, which had cost me so many white nights. Mounet offered me a delicious coffee, heard me read, and made many objections; then he added that, for the moment, verse in the theater seemed to be on the decline, that the classics seemed to continue to thrive barely, that he himself was feeling weary of the battle, and that he was planning to dedicate himself to sculpture. He showed me several of his attempts: a head of Saint John the Baptist, a bust. He invited me to come, every Sunday, to take coffee with him, and meanwhile he continued marvelously to play Orestes or Orosmane,[25] the Cid or Hernani,[26] and to recite pretty verse that my friend Grangeneuve has called *Triolets to Nini*. I put together a second piece in verse; I came to read it to Mounet, who (yes, yes, I remember it well) fell soundly asleep between the fourth and fifth scenes of the second act. I put an end, then and there, to my dramatic attempts at the quai de Gesvres, contenting myself with the excellent dominical mocha, and no longer speaking like a poet, but like a simple and modest Perigordian, happy to open up with one of the most illustrious of compatriots.

One evening, as I was recounting my misadventure at the indistinct restaurant where the sons of Périgord gathered, one of them, a young lawyer, M. Rousset, said to me: "But the actor Saint-Ger-

---

[25]Orosmane: a character in the play *Zaïre*, by Voltaire.

[26]Hernani: the main character in the eponymous drama by Victor Hugo.

main is also a Perigordian, from Thiviers or Excideuil."

One morning, equipped with the fatal roll, I appeared at Saint-Germain's apartment, 15, rue Pigalle.

"Monsieur," I said to the very spiritual comedian, "it's as an author of course, but also, and above all, as a compatriot that I present myself to you."

Saint-Germain looked at me dumbfounded.

"I know," I added, "that that title is shared by several hundreds of thousands of men; but I have nothing else to offer, and I put it out there."

It is to be noted that I was speaking Gascon atrociously, and that the most intense Midi colored my syllables. Saint-Germain did not flinch, but asked me to leave the manuscript for him to read, and to come back in one week for a response.

I was on time for the rendez-vous, and I had the joy of hearing Saint-Germain say that it was quite good, and that he would do all he could to have me interpreted. Ravished, I burst out in Gascon, more than was usual for me:

"Thank you, my dear compatriot."

Saint-Germain, without laughing, said to me:

"Ah! that! but you do know that I was born on rue Soufflot, right?"

My friend the lawyer had made an error: his Saint-Germain was not the real Saint-Germain. My play, besides, was never put on: Saint-Germain fell ill, then he fell out with the actress who was going to play the principal role, then he quit the theater where he was to enter another; and then... and then... It sufficed that I had called Saint-Germain a compatriot for the bad luck to attach itself to our plans: no prophet is accepted in his own country!

Montigny, who had read the piece, threw his arms up towards the friezes, asking how in the world I had had the audacity to treat of a like subject. It had to do with a *Fils de fille*.[27] Alas! In that same gymnasium, several years later, Albert Delpit was able to have the

[27]*Fils de fille*: The son of a prostitute.

Son of Coralie put on without protests; and, here and there, such au-
dacities have been tolerated such that my poor play today, sleeping
in a box, has the effect on me of an essentially *old school* pastoral.

Then I succumbed to melancholy. The ministry of finance
was wearing me down, and literary life remained closed to me. Also,
it was an unqualifiable life that took hold of me. I went along,
culling love, or what looked like love, in the brasseries, in the artist
studios. Tamar was the goddess at that bizarre period of time. Tamar
was actually named Joanna or Nini, depending on the setting. That
girl, with an irreproachable physique, had been sold very young to
that special industrialist who went by the name of Gaetana de Marco,
and who trafficked in little Italian girls destined to pose *nude* in the
studios of the School of Fine Arts and elsewhere. That Nini-Joanna,
having posed for the painting done by Cabanel, which can be found
at the Luxembourg: *Tamar and her Brother Absalom*, held on to the
Biblical name of Tamar, which didn't prevent her from serving,
gracefully, bocks and Chartreuse in a small brasserie on rue Racine.
That brasserie was managed by a proud woman named Malvina, and
by a Polish man named Zukowski. There was a ground floor, where
passersby filled themselves up on beer and nutriment; but there was
also a entresol, where a piano groaned under the more or less skilled
fingers of students. Oh! how many times had Strauss, Métra, and
Fahrbach been skinned alive on that spinet! Above the entresol
reigned a furnished hotel, sometimes outrageously furnished. It was
there that my adventures with Nini-Joanna-Tamar unfolded. But, that
being part of my private life, I pass over it rapidly. It was at rue
Racine that I made the acquaintance of the illustrator Georges Lorin,
a charming watercolorist, since then having become a seductive
poet, and his inseparable friend, Maurice Rollinat.

Georges Lorin had just invented advertising cards, ornamented with a watercolor where chubby babies play with humanity. Does
anyone remember those first compositions? A nice poetry en-
wrapped the design. There were strange cavalcades of Cherubim on
dragonflies, enormous struggles between infants armed with bizarre
casques and holding swords longer than themselves: a phantasmago-
ria, an incredible and delicious evocation!

I knew Maurice Rollinat only by several pieces of verse published here and there.

But in front of that minuscule brasserie's eye-opening piano, it didn't take long for us to strike up an acquaintance. Sad and somber when alone, he became a gay companion when amongst us. And when the joyous and robust Normand Charles Frémine and the sfumato illustrator and kind poet Georges Lorin joined the party, we recited poems and sang songs, and, little by little, the wild Rollinat let himself go, and, then, striking wild chords, he affected the listeners' entrails by his rude voice, singing the music that was almost religious, composed by him to accompany sonnets by Baudelaire.

Gaunt, his face shadowed by thick rings of dark brown hair, eyes sunken under the arcade of his brow – his blue-green pupils – large mouth, strong mustache, ravaged face, tormented, grimacing, and his voice above all, that voice whose two octaves went in turn from exquisite tendernesses, to crazy caterwaulings, to gripping low notes: all that impressed us immensely and shook our nerves.

Only, soon, in that profane milieu, ironic gaiety gained the upper hand, and everything ended on crazy refrains, the most modest extract of which would terrify the chaste reader.

Then, when there was not too infernal a racket in the small brasserie, veritable seances of poetic diction were organized. One evening, even, a wretched bureaucrat, taking advantage of the fact that Maurice Rollinat was a city hall employee of the VIth arrondissement, and I myself being an attaché to the ministry of finance, ventured to declaim a sonnet in his fashion; his fashion was execrable; however, with an exquisite sense of politeness, each one of us lowered his head, dissimulating a fierce ennui, a bitter desolation that that awkward versification elicited in us. Unfortunately for the author, that silence intimidated him, and around the middle of the second tercet, instead of saying what he had written – *la magique palette* – his natural timidity, which he had made the huge mistake of overcoming for that occasion, regained the upper hand, and a slip of the neophyte's tongue made him pronounce this: *la pagique malette*. That was all it took. We doubled up in laughter. That Apollonian vengeance waged against a chance Marsyas was saved by unanimous applause. Only Charles Frémine, preserving his sang-froid, waited for the silence to be re-established and declared soberly: That's stupid!

Never again did that catechumen of the Muses expose himself to the hazards of diction.

One evening, on the small entresol, Rollinat and I found ourselves alone. We were talking literature, sharing some private stories.

I learned that he was the son of master Rollinat, Madame Sand's *Madagascan;* that the great novelist had been his godparent, and that she encouraged him in his debuts; that in his Berrichon countryside, savage and foggy, in that land, among its heath, a frightful fear seized men when faced with nature; that things took on melancholic and crazy aspects; he recited these rondels to me:

THE WOLVES

Brown and slender like nails,
They surprised me in the clearing,
And to the edge of a quarry
Followed me like two swindlers;

– Never the eye of jealous man
Had more murderous a glimmer;
Brown and slender like nails,
They surprised me in the clearing,

But hunger had made them mad,
For they crossed my barrier,
And there they were on their derrieres,
At my door! two large wolves,
Brown and slender like nails.

A vision perhaps of wandering dogs; but also an impression of dark solitude, of a deserted and terrifying landscape! As for passersby, vagabonds, they are the worst to encounter, in those desolate lands lacking in police officers and gas lamps.

THE SUSPECT GUEST

– We are quite alone at the base of this hill,
Quite alone! and midnight sounds with the old cuckoo!
The young stranger unnerves me a lot!
He leaves the fire, draws near, moves away,

Barely speaks a word, and never loudly:
– That individual plans a fatal blow! –
We are alone at the base of this hill,
Quite alone! and midnight sounds with the old cuckoo!

Oh! what I dream is horrible – My guest
Pursues the maid servant with an old halter...
I run! and a knife in his neck I plant,
Splattered with his brain that explodes...
– We are quite alone at the base of this hill.

The eleven-syllable lines employed there do not reveal their true value until the poem is declaimed by Maurice Rollinat; through that limping versification, he elicits the intensity of fear, the horrible fear with which the poet is struck in that Berrichon landscape that is so savage, but which he adores precisely because *he experiences the vertigo of terror!*

Around midnight, Maurice Rollinat said to me: "What do you say we shake our legs out a bit!" We exited, and after several walks up and down the boulevard Saint-Michel, he proposed to me that he improvise a little something to eat. We would go to his room, he had so many things he wanted to read to me, to recite to me, and bizarre melodies to bang out on his piano. A purchase of sausages, knuckles of ham, two bottles of wine, some bread, and there we were on our way to rue Saint-Jacques. Rollinat had a small lodging on the sixth floor.

Finished in short order the improvised meal! Rollinat opened his piano. That piano was a clavecin with antique, shrillish tones; obviously moaning for having been woken up so late, that instrument from the eighteenth century, by an artist from the end of the nineteenth. In place of minuets, poor spinet, instead of Vestris' light steps,[28] here's what it was forced to accompany, to Rollinat's funeral melody, the terrible sonnet that with bitter irony Baudelaire entitled *le Mort joyeux.*[29]

> *In a rich soil, and full of snails,*
> *I want to dig myself a deep grave*
> *Where I might stretch my bones, at leisure,*
> *And sleep in oblivion, like a shark in the wave.*
>
> *I hate testaments and I hate tombs!*
> *Rather than implore the world's tears,*
> *Living, I'd rather invite the crows*
> *To bleed every end of my filthy carcass!*
>
> *O worms, dumb, blind, dark companions,*
> *Here comes a free and joyous corpse,*
> *Epicurean philosopher, son of rot...*
>
> *Through my ruin, go then remorselessly,*
> *And tell me if there's still some torture*
> *For this old, soulless body, dead among the dead.*

Those who have only had Rollinat's written music before their eyes, those who have not heard that original, bizarre, and tormented artist moan two quatrains in a deep voice, vehemently throw out the first tercet, and terminate the second with a terrible cry of frightening anguish, cannot imagine the effect that that song produces, the first time one hears it.

Rollinat went through his repertoire almost in its entirety, then the verse of his volume *The Heathlands*, which he was preparing then for Sandoz and Fischbascher. At around seven in the morning, the poet read to me the scenario of an extraordinary drama that he needed to finish in collaboration with the kind Pierre Elzéar: strange partnership, which, moreover, came to nothing. Could it

---

[28]Vestris: possibly a reference to Gaétan Vestris (AD 1729-1808) or his son, Auguste Vestris (AD 1760-1842), both dancers.

[29]*le Mort Joyeux*: The Joyful Dead.

have ended any other way? The reader will have to judge for himself by the scenario itself, which has remained sufficiently engraved in my frightened memory.

At the lifting of the curtain, one saw a public square, towards dawn, a milling crowd, and a guillotine in the background. The victim toppled over, the blade fell; a terrifying "ah!" ran through the crowd, which, according to custom, retired painfully impressed, while a fleet wagon drove off into in the wings.

Standing, by himself, a man, M. A***, spoke: "Finally! I'm safe now! that innocent victim has satisfied my debt! God bless his soul!"

Suddenly, an individual, M. B***, carrying a suitcase, appeared, and went to knock on the door of a house: Bang! bang! bang!

The first gentleman spoke, in an aside: "Who knocks like that on the guillotined man's door?" Then, addressing himself to the man just arrived: "Monsieur, that house is closed, the unfortunate man who lived there has been executed just this very moment."

"Heavens!" exclaimed the other, "My brother! my brother! it is not possible!"

"His brother!" murmured M. A***, "Alas!"

And the brother of the guillotined man cried out: "My brother was innocent! I'm sure of it! I will find the guilty one!"

M. A***, alone, said to himself: "He will not find the guilty man; but I owe a reparation, if not to the guillotined man, alas! at least to the survivor, to that unfortunate brother."

In the second act, M. A***, very rich as a result of his crime, for which M. B***'s brother had been guillotined, gave, to repair his honor, his daughter and a large dowry to M. B***, who forgot in an instant of hymen his plans for vengeance against the true guilty party, and relegated the rehabilitation of his brother's name to a lower priority.

Some random incident at the end of the act obliged him to think about it again.

In the third act, M. B*** discovers finally the guilty man... his father-in-law! What will he do?

Here comes the denouement. M. A*** had the brother of M. B*** guillotined... M. B*** will force M. A***, his father-in-law, to guillotine himself in a room, and to save the honor of his children, that terrible denouement will be attributed to the madness of suicide.

Such was the dramatic scenario that Rollinat read to me after, I have to say, he had touched or charmed me by his poems, first lugubrious then crazily gay, funereal, or sometimes a bit sadistic.

But those vague evenings, those loves for models – o what physiques! – plunged the poor employee of the ministry of finance (126 fr. 25 c. per month) into ruin. Then, – oh! then! pity me! – I began to gamble. Yes! in strange gambling dens, I went to hazard my 126 fr. 25 c. on greasy, perhaps marked, cards! Yes! Near the Pantheon, a kind of brasserie with a secret basement opening its entrails to fawners on the Queen of Spades. During the afternoon, at the hour of absinthe, school functionaries, having arrived from diverse baccalaureate offices in the suburbs, could be found there, students of all sorts, perhaps butchers or grain merchants even; then, in the evening, a cosmopolitan crowd, all sorts, drunkards, and self-possessed fellows. Under the gleaming gas lamps, a certain monsieur cut the remarkable *bac*.[30] In dark corners, a poor man's *chemin de fer*[31] was set up. It was a factory at nine or at eight. I was winning at first, oh! naturally. Then, regularly, busted, the somber cleaning out of my thin wallet, the devourment of my winnings, sums borrowed of third parties, rare subsidies sent by a dreadful family who believed that a person can live, in Paris, at the end of the nineteenth century, on 126 fr. 25 per month, after two years a gratuitous supernumerary.

The bitter losses inspired me to defiances against the perpetual lucky bastards. We called them the *Greeks* in the old days, not that that distant nation, more than any other nation, to be honest, deserved that renown. Greeks! so be it!

---

[30]*bac*: baccarat, the card game.

[31]*chemin de fer*: French for "railroad": a card game.

Indignatio facit versum.[32]

Indignant, I wrote verses against the Greeks, blending notions from Homer, Saint John Chrysostom, and Greek roots, learnt at middle school, together with my rancors of an ultra-busted gambler, and from that resulted a humorous piece that had no great pretensions, that I began to recite, in the evenings, at dessert, when a sham Alicante or pseudo Champagne put a cap on thesis dinners in the Latin Quarter. That piece, spoken by me with an extraordinary Perigordian accent, gave me my first success. Ah! I didn't expect it at all, while composing it, any more than when I recited it, that that poem would be the point of departure of a literary life. I present it here by way of document, even though it has been published in *Flowers of Bitumen*;[33] [34] for "The Greeks" was what made me leave the dramatic path, to fall back into, for a long time thereafter, the abrupt, vast, and somber field of poetry:

THE GREEKS

One evening Æmilius, the prince of rotten luck,
Resolved to win – Mataia, vain thing –
Some talents with one of his Napoleons
In an obscure gambling den, not far from the Pantheon.
Night fell: Phoebe showed her timid face;
The player donned his woolen chlamys,
And to the den, where Ploutos presided over combats,
He sauntered, like the steers of Ajax, his feet in stockings.
The Greek temple opened its hideous postern
At the end of a corridor, true path to Avernus,
Where Phoebus-Apollo was represented
By a spent lantern in the acidic obscurity.
Æmilius entered under the plaster vault;
And suddenly an ephebe in a yellowish apron,
Who responded: "Vlaboum!" when one interrogates him,
Welcomed him on the sill. The crowd that was yelling

---

[32]*Indignatio facit versum*: Latin for "indignation makes [good] verse."

[33]Original footnote: One volume of poetry published by Ollendorff [in AD 1885].

[34]*Flowers of Bitumen: Fleurs du Bitume*, an English translation of which is available by Sunny Lou Publishing.

Stopped, contemplating the young proselyte;
But, as he did not have the look of a satellite,
The pensive Achaeans went back to their game.
A thick smoke filled the holy place with its stink.
Seated on tripods of austere craftsmanship,
The players held in their mouths a crater,[35]
And their lips emitted, by powerful expulsions,
Clouds of incense directed toward gaseous suns.

The ephebe was seen here and there in various groups:
On the marble tables he set down his his cups,
Glass amphora with solemn heads of foam,
Where yellow and white nectar frothed, hydromel
Which Gambrinus,[36] *Dionysus' old rival,*
Brews with hops and authentic barley.
On a zinc altar a thick-lipped Greek was enthroned,
Sticky like an old Priapus; but also stocky,
To whom, for this reason, all Diogenes' sons
Showed more respect than to the twelve gods of Athens.

Meanwhile, in the crowd, a cry rang out:
"Name of Zeus!" – Some big shot, having laid an egg,
                                   [clucked:
*"Cut! Cut! banker!" (*To cut! *verb of prey*
Whose future optative: I am going to win, is employed
With the verbal nine, *or the diminutive* eight;
And to do Charlemagne *is an infinitive,*
Whose present punters[37] *will be participles...*
Confer *Nieburh, passim, Burnouf: First principles)*
The punter Æmilius, pale, trembling, captivated,
Listens to that noise like a siren's song.

Several Thessalians with their stinking cnemides,
Subtle Argians, draped in their clamydes,

---

[35]crater: synecdoche for a cigar, when the lit end has a concave shape.

[36]Gabrinus: the mythical "patron saint" of beer, brewing, and all that goes with it.

[37]punter: a gambler, particularly one who bets against the bookmaker.

Bent over men come out of Sion, the Cretes
Escaping their native soil, above the straits,
Athletes who have no fear of the gods,
Daughters of Lesbos, women of Corinth,
Their trained fingers earning gold deniers
That the Boetians would offer to the god of fate,
And that, laughing quietly, garnered Perfidy.
The bank fleeced them, those pigeons of Arcadia!
Popoï! Æmilius didn't look at them;
He saw only the winners of combats,
And looked, – poor fool! – for the gold in his belt.
That nebulous temple, that impure atmosphere...
Everything excites him!... It is gold dancing joyously in his
                                                              [eyes!

The encephalon bursts into flame at a simple rubbing
Of your wheel, o Fortune!... Let's go! here's the prey!
Æmilius standing, approaches, and, full of joy,
Throws a metal coin onto the baize.
Adieu, dear silver sheep: here comes the butcher's block!

O degenerate Greeks! O sons of Themistocles!
If your ancestors of bronze came down from their pedestals,
And, leaving for a day the Champs-Elyseens,
Came to contemplate you, pale Athenians;
Those who spilt their blood in the Scamander's[38] waves,
Those who carried Alexander's glory far and wide,
Pheu! Pheu! what would they say if they saw their sacred
                                                              [name,

That name that is the pride of the Parthenon's walls,
That keeps the summits of Mt. Taygetus still standing
And the indigenous cohort of gods still in memory,
While it gives cover, like a vile, sweaty glad rag
To the outright theft of the knights?
Finding the allure of the word "Greek" ambiguous,
Socrates would drink his cup of hemlock again,
Old Demosthenes would spit out his pebbles,
And the prolix Isocrates would grow silent before you!

---

[38]Scamander: the ancient name of the river Menderes, in modern-day Turkey; it flows into the Aegean Sea.

O dead of Marathon! o soldiers of Salamis!
Marmorean heroes that ancient glory shines on!
Its with écarté[39] (from the Greek word écartaïos)
That your counterfeiters fleeced Æmilius.

Æmilius lost every last copper coin of his.

Poor Boetian whom fury makes drunk!
The Achaeans laughed! Æmilius sat down,
And, noticing his cup untouched, he grabbed it,
And, highly strung, broke the vessel on the ground.
Then, to pay for the damage, he left his petasus;
And casting an intense look at the Greek temple,
His heart full, he exited completely broke.
The player felt sick to the encranion;
He cursed under his breath his stupid escapade:
"I swear," he said, "by the subterranean gods,
I would like to hug you and break your back,
O Greeks!!!..." He addressed himself to the greedy Argians;
Too late! his hands patted his large, empty pockets:
Adieu, fields where Ilion once stood!
And he shook a fist at the walls of the Pantheon,
While the Scythians,[40] by order of the archons,
Came, at a measured pace, to arrest the punters.

That simple rhymed pleasantry did more for me than a huge
drama in verse about the war of 1870, than two comedies in verse,
than a drama in prose, than well-crafted, groomed, polished sonnets,
which I peddled here and there. O chance! I recited that piece at the
hour when, at the tables d'hôte, after a modest, but happy, meal, people asked to hear *something from everybody.* That was my dessert
song. I didn't attach much importance to it, dreaming of better, o
ambition! when one evening a young man, an enraged republican,
who was founding a political journal in the Latin Quarter, asked me
for that verse, to publish it in an issue, his first number. Someone

---

[39]écarté: a two-handed card game.

[40]Original footnote: The archers charged with the responsibility of keeping the
peace in Athens were also called "Scythians."

was asking me for my verse! Finally! Ask yourself whether I gave it to him.

But here occurs an absolutely unexpected incident. Immediately after the publication of that versified joke, the Greek colony in Paris, the entire Hellenic community, including those attached to the legation, the civil and the military attachés, were upset; a reunion took place, during the course of which severe motions were discussed. I had a lot of trouble putting out that fire. I was aided by the painter Kalloudis, a Hellene who took courses at the School of Fine Arts; by Duc-Quercy, who, before being an emeritus socialist, was a professor, and counted among his pupils a throng of young Greeks; and principally by M. de S***, ancient plenipotentiary minister to Athens, who demonstrated to those good patriots that I had nowise tried to insult the young Hellas, whose sympathy for France and courage were admirably demonstrated in the cruel hours of 1870.

That adventure had an unexpected outcome: which was that I became at that point a regular at the Turco-Greek restaurant, that the cashier, a tall blonde... no, I will not say it, that's my private life again. What do you want from me? I lived across the street.

Soon, I wrote a follow-up to "The Greeks," with this title: "The Romans." The girls from the Eternal City have never sent me a cartel, and I regret it.

Chapter Five

*The desert. – Fumism and the ministry. – Deaf by persuasion. – Praise
for the joke. – Tamar. – Guy Tomel. – Nina's birthday party. –
Necrological article. – Memories of rue des Moines: comical dramas by
Villiers de l'Isle-Adam.*

The Latin Quarter was becoming at that time something of a small
desert. Richepin had left it to go and live in Montmartre, Bouchor
made only rare appearances, Bourget confined himself to his work;
Guy de Maupassant, who, under the pseudonym of Guy de Valmont,
had just published his first poem in *The Republic of Letters*, had
turned to prose, and frequented assiduously Émile Zola in the
evenings, after spending the day at the office in the ministry of the
navy.

Here are the first lines of verse published by Guy de
Maupassant, under his pseudonym of Guy de Valmont:

A RAY OF SUNLIGHT

It was the month of June. Everyone seemed to celebrate.
Crowds circulated, boisterous and carefree,
I don't know why but I was happy too, really;
That noise, like drunkenness, had gone to my head.

The sun was exciting bodily powers in me;
It entered completely into the core of my being;
And I felt boiling in me those passions
That the first sun birthed in the heart of Adam.

A woman passed by; she looked at me,
I don't know what fire her eyes shot at me,
With what transports my soul was seized;
But it came on me suddenly, like a frenzy,
To throw myself at her, a furious desire
To hold her in my arms and kiss her mouth!
A cloud of blood, red, covered my eyes,
And I thought of holding her in savage embrace.

I embraced her, pleaded with her, threw her down;
Then, lifting her up suddenly with a powerful effort,
I kicked off the earth, and, into space
Streaming with sunlight, in a bound I carried her.
We went through the sky, body to body, face to face,
And, ever towards the blazing star, I climbed,
Pressing her to my chest in so strong an embrace
That, in my clenched arms, I found she was dead.

Maurice Rollinat, who had just published his volume *The Heathlands* the day before, on May 15, disastrous and truly anti-literary hour, had departed for the countryside, jaundiced with despair. *The Republic of Letters* had moved to rue de Châteaudun, far from the Sherry-Cobbler, and the Sherry-Cobbler passed away under an avalanche of *papiers timbrés*.[41]

Georges Lorin and I, we were melancholic in the evenings, and we went to sit down at a table, pensive, in the small entresol on rue Racine. Politics whirled around us in violent conversations: the Duke de Broglie and M. de Fourtou seemed at that time inevitably more famous than any Homer or V. Hugo. The bitter discussions on the 363[42] followed us to the restaurant, to the café, to the brasserie. Georges Lorin found them again at his studio, rue Madame, with Testut and Massin, the great entrepreneurs of chromolithography; as for myself, I felt them smoldering under the terrorized silence of the employees at the ministry.

That was a lamentable period, when it seemed that never, never ever, would anyone be occupied with literature again. It was to be renounced. But from my frequentations with the illustrious Sapeck, I had conceived of *fumism*, a sort of disdain for everything, an internal contempt for beings and things, which translated itself on the outside into innumerable attacks, farces, and *fumisteries*. In the silence of the finance ministry, I played my hand. That was a terrible and joyful period.

---

[41]papiers timbrés: literally stamped papers: fiscal taxes.

[42]363: a reference to the "manifesto of the 363" Republican deputies to the president of the Republic, MacMahon, in AD 1877.

I was at that time an employee in the great gallery of Annuities; I no longer checked things off, I paid out sums instead, without being paid any more for that. One day, a big, slender bloke, long, pasty, entered the office. He was the new boy. Someone came and reported to me what that debutant had said about me; he had said: "I'm going to see close up then that curious animal that calls himself a poet!"

Capital! Here are, more or less, the terms with which I received him, with the greatest seriousness:

"Allow me, sir and dear confrere, to salute you in the name of astral circumvallation, whose serene, adequate, but illusory monetary appreciation adds soot to space and leaves us however to live in good amity with the gastropods that chance happens to send our way."

The other stood dumbfounded. Then, profiting from a minute of respite, he went to ask everyone in the gallery if I wasn't fit to be tied. My comrades, getting caught up on what had just happened, reported to him that, on the contrary, I shined with incredible clarity.

For the duration of the time that I had relations with that ephebe, I employed the same language:

"Please, I beg you, sir and dear colleague, if however the sinuous and paraphrastic ingenuity of cosines permits it, and if, by pluvial onomatopoeias, whose infrangible and penetratory circulus pours down on contemporary aridity the vitreism of spaces, if finally the substantiation of oneiric desires should come true, please hand me the statement of account number 2 from the expenses chapter."

In the eyes of that poor boy a depth of terror was revealed, and, as he appeared not to understand, I shouted at him in a stentorian voice:

"Are you deaf, man with the cruel beard? Would that a rapid mental initiator perforate deep within your mellifluous Eustachian tube!"

Little by little, a conspiration was hatched to make that unfortunate man really believe he was deaf. But what persuaded him of it was the following adventure:

Someone pasted onto the window of his office the following notice, in enormous letters:

"Warning: Speak loudly, the comptroller is absolutely deaf."

It must be explained, to start, that, for the payment of revenues, a person must present himself before a first window above which is inscribed this word: *Payer;* then one passes to the following window: *Comptroller*. There, one is obliged to wait until a special office task is completed. Then, at the end of a more or less long period of time, one presents himself at the following window: *Cashier*.

At each of these stations, the payer, the comptroller, and the cashier asks the annuitant: "How much have you withdrawn?" It's a means to avoid human errors. That's done in a discreet voice, calmly, as if one were thinking out loud quietly.

That day then, when the Public Warning was affixed, this happened: the first annuitant to present himself to the payer responded to the question: 'How much have you withdrawn?" by a figure, 753 fr. 25. The payer then said to him: "Go to the comptroller's window." Waiting there, idly, for a minute or two, the annuitant noticed the Warning, and when the comptroller finally opened his window, asking in turn: "How much have you withdrawn?" There was a terrible voice, when, filling his cheeks and cupping his hands to his mouth, the annuitant hurled: "Seven hundred fifty-three francs, twenty-five centimes."

The stupefaction of the comptroller was great, all the more so when the same annuitant, so unexpectedly taken with the need to shout, after having passed to the next window, responded to the same question in a very soft voice.

There were also others who presented themselves throughout the day. That stirred up the entire gallery, and the poor man asked: "Why are they all screaming like that?"

I responded to him: "Sir and dear colleague, the argentoid impetration whose viscera is shaken vociferates through laryngiform fissures, in order from there to tympanize, vibratory, the stooges of

3

the gabelle."

Towards evening, the head of payments, who has no authority over the employees of comptroller's unit, came passing by, heard the annuitants' loud voices, approached, then, having read the placard, went to inquire of the comptroller unit head, who, after consultation, rushed into the office, speaking in a natural voice, addressing him to the other employees:

"Alright, alright! what's going on here?"

Then, leaning into ear of the comptroller, and yapping, he said to him:

"When one has an infirmity of this type, one let's his boss know, and he does not perform a service that involves contact with the public; I am going to reassign you to our central office tomorrow."

And so it came about. Let no one think however that the service had been slowed down by these jokes; the service on its own takes a long time without the employees being able to do anything about it. But the employees of the State cashier's office, I say this sincerely, being under the public eye, in glass cages, acquit themselves as quickly as they can of their duty, all the more certain that the quicker they conclude their business, the sooner the public can go on its way. One must trust me on this. As for offices not in the public eye, I cannot say the same.

Those pranks and many others like them were able to distract for a moment; but there was nothing literary about it. If I cite that anecdote, it's to make it felt just how that generation, which had so many reasons for being pessimistic, struggled for gaiety against the afflictions of boredom and jaundice. Later on, at the Hydropaths Club, as well as at the Chat Noir, it was always, together with the often Schopenhauerian literary and artistic outbursts, in large part in order to release spleen. And honestly, after all the setbacks in the beginning, I owe Sapeck a votive candle for having initiated me into that interior madness, which translates itself on the exterior by imperturbable buffooneries.

The too great seriousness of young artists, the *pontificate,* is,

I think, bad hygiene. What harm is there, in their twentieth year, for men, following the good advice of Ernest Renan, to give themselves over to joy?

If it sounds here like I'm pleading attenuating circumstances, perhaps it is true: many among us have since been reproached for a crazy attitude, wild conduct, bizarre behavior, laughter, and large outbursts of gaiety. That was a crime in our sweet country of France! Strange! I say it for the record, without rancor, and if I had to do it all over again, I would act in the same way. Better to stay alive thanks to insouciance, than to be dead stoically for misery, draping oneself in a Byronian hero's coat. If sometimes we exceeded the bounds permissible to laughter, at least we didn't have to light Escousse's stove[43] or look for Gerard de Nerval's scarf.[44] That's something.

Better to be a churl standing than an emperor under ground!

On the other hand, that practice of dry humor, those staged fumist attempts, gave a certain aplomb to that provincial whose timidity was in great need of it.

Oh! to be sure, I had already shed several illusions as a result of rubbing shoulders with poets. They no longer appeared titanic, no, no, no! They were beings who drank, ate, moved, loved in an ordinary fashion; nevertheless, they seemed to possess in themselves an extraordinary confidence that I found superior. Evidently, it was the inferiority of their neighbors that made them appear so great. And me, *ed'io anché,* I could grow in front of my inferiors, and annoy them, and keep them under control. That gave me a certain allure. All the same – admire the contradiction! – I always felt a vague remorse after making fun of the weak and small. A natural goodness – a simple kindness! – forced me to feel sorry for them. I even made excuses to that poor devil of a comptroller I had given a hard time to.

From then on, was born in me, instead of a hatred of society, a hatred that I could have conceived against the holders of publicity,

---

[43]Escousse: Victor Escousse (AD 1813-1832) a French dramatic author who took his own life after several failed dramas.

[44]Gerard de Nerval's scarf: de Nerval hanged himself.

against the egoists who considered only themselves and their comrades, according to that axiom by the poet Gilbert: "No one will have wit, besides us and our friends!" instead of a fury against the present poor state of *chance;* yes, there was born in me a tenderness for humble poets who, poor disgraces of the ideal, knock themselves out in unknown garrets. To see so many geniuses of all sorts come out easily into the sunlight, thanks to the complicity of comraderies, I looked up at the rooves also, at the lit windows on the seventh floors above the entresol, wondering perhaps whether an unknown genius didn't struggle there against the difficulty of making an appearance, in the dark clouds of the Unpublished. I believed I could hear a voice cry out to those Prometheuses of our Caucasian attics: You will remain in the shadows for perpetuity!

And imagining to myself that a great many forces were lost in that way, I became an apostle. Oh! dream! I would have wished to open wide all the doors of an imaginary and grandiose theater to those poets thirsty for glory. The idea of the theater of the *hydropaths* must have its origin there. Let's move on.

Tamar, unfaithful mistress, had failed to appear at multiple rendezvous, one among others, on Mardi Gras. Where had she run off to, the statue? Probably towards some Élysée-Montmartre. I wrote to her in verse, which is the culmination of vengeance.

Some time later, as she had not responded to me, either because she had nothing in fact to say to me, or because she distrusted with good reason her spelling, for spelling was, for her, quite inferior to her body, it goes without saying! sometime afterwards, I resolved, after having forewarned her, to pay her a visit, rue du Montparnasse.

She lived there, with a kind of witch who acted as her domestic and *adviser*. I pushed aside the duenna, and rushed into the small room, where an unexpected scene stopped me in my tracks, stunned, standing, the very image of despair.

Tamar, half-naked, sitting on cushions before a coke-burning fire, was strumming a guitar. Sequins in her hair, a collar of imitation pearls around her naked neck, her eyes lost in the distance, a cigarette sticking out of the corner of her mouth, she shook the shrill chords out of that Spanish torture instrument. Here, there, seraglio pastilles burned, letting out a strong odor of incense and musk. That's her, naturally, whom I noticed at first. But, farther away, a young gentleman, holding an umbrella between his knees, on which he had placed his round hat, looking as though he had fallen into a state of half ecstasy.

After my having cast exasperated looks at the beautiful Tamar, who, impassive, continued strumming the chords of her guitar, o torture! I stared at the guest of that seraglio, o pastilles! He looked at me too; then, addressing himself to Tamar, he said:

"Is that the fellow who sent you the poetry?"

She made a sign: yes, with her head, balancing at the end of her lips her cigarette that was beginning to go out – a single and vague indication of a contained emotion, oh! very contained.

Then, the young gentleman rose, took his umbrella in one hand, his hat in the other, and bowing courteously before me, he said:

"Let's not be ridiculous, alright? I would like to have two words with you on the balcony. There!"

"Gladly," I responded.

We passed over to the balcony; and, after he had closed the double doors behind us, the young gentleman said to me:

"I have read with great interest the poetry that you sent to Nini-Tamar. I would not want, for anything in the world, to hamper a love such as you have depicted; and rather than cut the throat of a poet, I prefer to give you free rein, if you're so minded."

"Humph! humph!" I said.

"To go to cuffs would be absurd! That girl is not worth the honor you do her, loving her like a goddess..."

"Let's stop right there, " I said to him. "I am ridiculous, so much the worse for me; but it will pass. Let's go back inside, and I will retire in five minutes, that's all I will give myself to make a testament internally of that great love."

We went back inside. Tamar hid her uneasiness under the frenetically guitaresque chords. Our silence accompanied her, enveloped her.

As I got up to leave, the young gentleman said to me:

"We are going to exchange cards, no?"

"Gladly."

Under Tamar's uneasy eye, the two heroes exchanged cards.

"May I come to visit you tomorrow?" said the young gentleman.

"Perfect."

And I took my leave, reading this on the card of my successor: "GUY TOMEL, Man of Letters." The following morning, despite Nini-Tamar's supplications, Guy Tomel deserted his odalisque's bed and showed up at my place:

"You're not upset with me," he asked.

"The night brings healing," I replied.

"Excellent!" added Guy Tomel, "I'm happy for that bizarre coincidence that gives me the opportunity to make your acquaintance; for I suppose that if you sent to studio models poems that seemed exquisite to me, you ought to have composed others, and it's in order to read them that I've come."

"But I'm a theatrical author," I exclaimed.

"Come now, you must have written lots of verse; don't pretend."

I let that Guy the Conqueror leaf through my drawers. His examination was favorable; because he declared to me that if I didn't published a volume of verse in the near future I was an poor wretch."

Thus I found, by chance, a man who, authoritatively, yanked me away from dramas, comedies, and vaudevilles, to threw me back into poetry again.

Guy Tomel was a professor; he was also, in my eyes, a bit of a prophet. I thank him for it, without thanking him too much for it, for there are times when I would have much preferred to have become a writer of operettas. Well!

Everything is connected to something else.

One evening, Georges Lorin declared to me that he was growing tired of Odeon, that there was an omnibus, unique in the world: Batignolles-Clichy-Odéon, indicating by his description even that a link exists between those distant localities; that, what's more, it was Tuesday, and that on Tuesday, Madame Nina de Villard, assisted by her very lovely mother, Madame Gaillard, received poets, painters, sculptors, and musicians, not to mention dilettantes solely interested in listening to the artists while consuming some beers or several punches.

There was a celebration that evening, a great celebration, in the small mansion on rue des Moines where Nina de Villard lived, simply Nina, as her friends called her. It was her birthday; bright lights, Venetian lanterns, fireworks, songs, poems, music, a throng of poets and artists come to applaud the comedy and greet the beautiful Nina, who, smiling, graceful, in her *flesh-and-blood* dress, passed by shining, handing out handshakes, with her so fine little hand. The beautiful birthday celebration of Nina, about which later, when her spirit began to grow dark, when she referred to herself as *the dead woman*, she said: "That was the most beautiful day of my life!"

On that day showed up those even who no longer frequented the hospitable salon on rue des Moines: François Coppée, Racot, Anatole France, Léon Valade, Camille Pelletan, Catulle Mendès, Jean Richepin, Germain Nouveau, Paul Alexis, Coquelin cadet, Villiers de l'Isle-Adam, the three Cros, Marcellin Desboutins, Henry Ghys, and many others that I forget: the very strange necromancer and magician Delaage, the apocalyptic musician Cabaner, and de Sivry,[45] musician also, but more of a cabalist shod with occult science, the eccentric Toupier-Bézier, and the intransigent Bazire, and the reactionary Léo Montancey, and the good giant Boussenard, and his brother the voyageur Louis Boussenard, and the sailor des Es-

---

[45]de Sivry: Charles de Sivry, see Léon Bloy's (positive) impression of him as a musician and artist in *Words of a Demolitions Contractor*, Sunny Lou Publishing, 2020. He was also Paul Verlaine's brother in law.

sarts, and the illustrator Forain, etc., etc.

Among the women who attended that celebration, I will cite Mesdames Augusta Holmès, the poet-composer; Marie de Grandfort, assiduous editor of *la Vie Parisienne*; Mme. de Rute, who was still Mme. Rattazzi; Mme. Lhéritier, and others, and still others.

That was Nina's radiant period, the culminating point of her life as a pretty woman and eminent artist. Rich, she was all smiles: accomplished musician, she had solicited bravos, while performing both great works by the masters as well as her own polished compositions. Then, from music to poetry, her fine mind took a single bound. At that time, it was rue Chaptal at first, then rues de Londres and de Turin; she had opened a salon visited by all that artistic Paris, young and fresh, had great hopes for. Finally, rue des Moines, in that mansion where I saw her, she continued opening her hospitable house to lyric poets, happy and sad, musicians, painters, those taken by art and fantasy, so enthusiastic herself and taken with the clatter of laughter and the sonority of beautiful songs. Giddy and joyful epoch! when death itself, – death, which had already taken a large swath from the milieu I'm talking about: Chatillon, Racot, Cabaner, Léon Valade, Léo Montancey, my very dear father – death was sung by Nina, who so sadly would have to die herself, having lost her dream and her soul at the bottom of some dark well. Here's the testament that she wrote at that time, so near still and so far away:

> *TESTAMENT*
>
> *I don't want to be buried – In a sad cemetery;*
> *– I want to be in a greenhouse, – And have artists*
> *come visit me.*
>
> *Henri must promise me – To make my statue*
> *in white marble, – And Charles[46] swear on his head –*
> *To cover it with diamonds.*
>
> *The bas-reliefs will be in gilded bronze. –*
> *They will represent – The three Jeanne, then*
> *Cleopatra, – And then Aspasia and Ninon.*

---

[46]Original footnote: Henri... Charles: The sculptor Henri Cros, the poet Charles Cros.

Have my mass sung at Notre-Dame, – For it's
Victor Hugo's cathedral; – And make the draperies
be white like women, – And have someone play the
piano.

That mass must be done by a young man –
Without a published work but who has talent. – I
would like it a lot – If the singer was his lover.

Finally it must be a small gathering – In the
news for one week. – On earth, alas! for I'm bored, –
I'll need to go and amuse myself elsewhere.

That was the period when, to her mother, Mme. Gaillard, so
good beneath her irony, so charming and like an ancestor from the
XVIIIth century, indulgent and spiritual, she addressed this comical
and tender dizain, after some vague scolding no doubt:

TO MAMA

Go, never hope to resemble those mothers
Who, Ambiguously, cause bitter tears to flow;
You are not solemn, and you will not know
How to curse with the haughty gesture of a forearm;
You have never sewn, never attended to my linen,
You spend less time with me than with your ape;
But, despite that, on evenings of good humor,
It's with you I will laugh with all my heart;
Together we will run first promenades,
For I find you the most chic of comrades.[47]

I recall how I was received in that house, and how my timidity disappeared little by little. Verse was recited, and the applause as
well as the criticism by Nina were spot on. There, I recited *The
Greeks, The Romans*, and quite a few other poems; little by little, I
got rid of my terrible Gascon accent; instead of seeming to chew on
live coals and iron, I taught myself, in the company of musicians,
poets, and declaimers of new verse, to soften the barbarous tones, to
discipline the wild syllables.

---

[47]Original footnote: *Fueillets Parisians*, posthumous volume by Nina de Villard.

It is in that artistic salon of Nina that I thus waged my first battle veritably, and I really owed this homage, here, to the poor dead woman. Some people, who scarcely knew her, attacked her with bitter criticisms in journal articles, and none of those who could respond, having a ready tribune, did it. And even, when she was led to the cemetery – ah! not as she had wanted it in her testament, not as a *small celebration*! no – there were hardly more than twenty of us. As articles thrown in the guise of flowers on her grave, she barely got more than this, what a friend from suffering bad days wrote, after returning from that lamentable ceremony.

NINA DE VILLARD

She was buried in her Japanese dress. The first time I saw her, she was wearing it; it was a black satin piece of clothing, embroidered all over with bright and marvelous flowers, bought for her in Yeddo.[48] *She had on the top of her head, amassed in a thick knot, her admirable dark hair, smooth and shiny; bright and bizarre pins, of the same provenance as the dress, created a kind of aureole around her chignon. I was struck by the beauty of her pale and calm face: her velvety eyes, the shape of her nose, the grace of her smile, created a harmonious whole, peaceful, almost severe, that contrasted with the somewhat loud flash of her eccentric toilette.*

She had just been painted in that costume: half reclining on a low sofa, surrounded by flowers and fans. She displayed a infantile joy. That was the magnificent period of her life, the memory of which re-animated her spirit, during the three troubled years preceding her death. Everything dated from then. – "I was beautiful, then," she used to say melancholically... "I was beautiful because I was happy..." And the past came back to her in a thousand little intimate details, tender or joyous, that brought life back into her eyes and her smile.

When she was in good health and surrounded

---
[48]Yeddo: Edo, Japan.

by people, I saw little of her, despite the very vivid sympathy her remarkable intelligence and her artistic tastes inspired in me; there were too many people in that little mansion on rue des Moines for an intimacy to be established between us. – It was later, when I learnt she was ill, that I saw her again and became her friend; – I visited her every day for six months.

When I met her again on rue Notre-Dame-de-Lorette, at that same house from which the funeral procession departed, Nina no longer wished to leave her bed. I can still see her. She had done her toilette a little to receive me. A blue-silk shirt garnished with white lace, a hint of powder on her cheeks, and her always beautiful hair well combed around her face. She had hardly changed in appearance. No visible sign of the illness that would take her away. She called herself the dead woman, and often that upsetting phrase returned to her discolored lips:

When I was alive. – *'When I was alive, I loved this and that; I wore light-hearted dresses and big hats with falling feathers... People came to see me... They found me beautiful, – I was loved. – Now that I'm dead, people leave me alone, I frighten them... and I have nothing to wear.'*

When we came to make her get out of bed, there were evenings when the Nina of yesteryear appeared almost whole again with her fine gaiety, her admirable understanding of artistic things, and the calm, easy, and correct attitude with which she knew how to turn a phrase; if, on my insistence, she sat down at the piano, – she had lost nothing of her former talent; her small narrow, tapered hands, ran swiftly over the clavier like tamed birds; if, around the large table, one sat down to compose verse or end rhymes, Nina's improvisation was always the best and promptest. I kept what she composed one evening. She was already rather ill and had had a vi-

*olent crisis during the day; – in order to distract her,
I begged her to write some lines – she leaned over the
table, took up a piece of paper and composed the following lines of verse:*

> *Venus today wears an azure stocking
> And at Marcelin's place[49] she tells stories;
> She looks deeply into the reflection of the waves,
> In the so-pure green of her large clear eyes
> Under their black lashes, of her motherland.
> When people see her pass on the boulevard,
> A goddess escaped from her pedestal
> And coming to grace them with her presence,
> They wish to erect altars to her,
> But she responds that that bores her
> And that she allows poor mortals
> To speak slang in her company.*

*Nobody, besides, knew how to listen like she
did, even in her last years. Sitting in an armchair, a
placid expression on her face, her body sagging a bit,
she listened to everything and was the first to understand the least nuances that someone said; when Villiers de l'Isle-Adam read to her one of his stories, or
Émile Goudeau one of his new poems, with an admirable judgment she savored and analyzed immediately the beauties or the weaknesses. –* I am a woman
taken by beautiful things, *she wrote somewhere. One
cannot sum her up, or say it, any better.*

*People have spoken a great deal about her sa-
lon, of those who were found there, who made a stop
there along the way, while waiting for fortune or
fame; – but as for her, she was judged cruelly and su-
perficially, – some have gone beyond what is permissible even. Men are not gentle with women, nor indulgent – nor grateful. – The ingratitude that was
shown to her surpassed everything one could imagine, and she must have suffered more terribly than*

---

[49]Original footnote: *La Vie parisienne.*

she wanted to admit: some say she died from it, and that her malady began right after a hateful article was written against her; – I don't believe it – the crack must have existed prior to then; without that, would she have really despaired so? In good health, and sane mind, she would have taken it in stride – after an hour of irritation, a profound forgetfulness.

It was a great pity for everyone and an immense sorrow for her friends to have watched the darkening of so delicate and so elevated an intelligence. Death, which she summoned, with her hands joined, her eyes filled with tears, with cries so piercing and such passionate refusals, came finally. I have loved and esteemed Nina enough not to lament her having left this earth before us. – There were not a lot of us standing around her casket – not a great number of us around her desolate mother... If all those who owe her something however had been there, the attendance would have been considerable. Listed below are the most ingrateful among those who became famous. They no longer visited her, so be it – but they owed her that last visit.

Over there, in the dark house where she remained for two days, rose-colored silk stalkings and satin shoes were placed on her little feet – she was dressed, according to her last wishes, in her Japanese dress, satin fabric embroidered with brilliant flowers, witness to the joys that escaped and a past that had stayed alive in her ill head – her hands of a woman, of a poet, of a musician were laid across her chest, – her thick black hair was combed over her forehead. The traces of her last sufferings, last battles, her supreme despair, disappeared in the calm of death; Nina displayed the beauty of her youth once again, which she lamented with such bitterness and such poignant regrets.

– Marie de Grandfort.

In the end, in fact, her existence had been as dark as the years were joyous when I came to sit down at the hospitable table in her house on rue des Moines. That name of Moines reminds me of a crazy scenario, the extravagant piece that Nina had composed in collaboration with Richepin, I believe, and Germain Nouveau, a strange drama where this epic line of verse can be found:

Everyone calls me Didier, I call myself Enguerrand.

I still see, from the gay period, old Châtillon reciting *la Levrette en paletot*, and I hear from here the terrible voice of Toupier-Béziers, proclaiming:

"Yes, my son, I wished to be a swallow fluttering above the quarriers, I drank the air and the light; but one must be a bee! You see, wings don't suffice! Today, I am nothing more than an old salad bowel without a salad!..."

Nina, softly, interrupted that thunder:

"What are you doing? but what are you doing there? What are you doing, Emilios? (That was my name then.) Why are you torturing Toupier?"

I excused myself as best I could, pretexting that, led by my accursed Hispano-Italo-Greek accent, I had called the poet Toupier: Toupiéro-Béziéro!

And then laughter, Toupier first.

It was there also when Villiers de l'Isle-Adam, the refined artist of *Nouveau-Monde*, *Azraël*, and *Contes cruels*, uttered with a Satanic expression and a silent laugh, the following little dramas:

First drama: The scene is a room with a bed; in the bed, a woman writhes; around her, everything necessary to give birth: a doctor, a midwife, vases, bowls, flasks; an insipid odor. The child only barely shows its head; it opens its eyes, looks at the scene, then cries out: "So this is it, life! Oh!" And goes back inside.

Second drama: A gentleman, very exasperated, armed with large knives, leaps out of a fiacre, goes into a house, mounts the staircase, breaks open a door. On a bed, a gentleman and a lady are in the act of making love. The intruder plants his knives so abruptly, that he transpierces the couple, crying: "Miserable wretches!" Then, he turns them over; stupefied, he contemplates them, and says: "Oh! oh!"

He'd come to the wrong floor.

How many fine hours were spent there, listening to austere music, or poems, or nonsense.

Adieu, poor Nina!

I don't want to be buried
In a sad cemetery;
I want to be buried in a greenhouse,
And have artists visit me.

She has her grave covered in flowers now, in Montmartre cemetery, near the artists, and I send her these lines, like a supreme visiting card.

Chapter Six

Charles Cros: Le Coffret de santal. *- The inventor. – The monologues. – André Gill:* la Muse à Bibi. *– The publisher's research.* – The Flowers of Bitumen.

It was to Nina that *le Coffret de santal* was dedicated, a volume in verse written by the poet Charles Cros. Poet and also mathematician, inventor of a bunch of chemical things, color photography among them; but inventor also of the monologue, such was Charles. Face of a Hindu, curly hair, thin black mustache, swarthy complexion. Witty, gay, spirited, and at the same time scientific, a dreamer, an observer. Rarely has a man been more gifted. He had for patrons and scientific protectors the Duke de Chaulnes and the Count de Montblanc, and the Academy awarded him a prize for his volume of verse *le Coffret de santal.*

Oh, there was the song of the Chinese poet Li Bai, or the poem about Gottlieb, with this verse in refrain:

Hou! hou! hou! the wind blows in the branches[50]

There was also the ballad of the archer:

She had beautiful blonde hair
Like autumn moss, so long
That it fell to her heels.

And others still, sad or perverse sonnets, white or withered visions, pink or black:

With Flowers, with Women,
With Absinthe, with Fire,
One can entertain oneself a little,
Play one's role in some drama.

Absinthe, drunk on a winter's eve,
Shines a green light into the smoky soul;

---

[50]*L'Orgue*, dedicated to André Gill.

And Flowers, on the dearly beloved,
Smell sweet before the bright Fire.

Then, kisses lose their charm,
Having lasted several seasons;
Reciprocal betrayals ensure
That one day one leaves without tears.

One burns letters and bouquets,
And the Fire is put in the alcove;
And, if the sad life remains intact,
There's still Absinthe and its bouquets...

The portraits are consumed by the flames...
The clenched fingers are trembling...
One dies for having slept too long a time
With Flowers, with Women.

That poet is eminently complex. One of his biographers said this of him:

"At eleven years old, Charles Cros is taken with Oriental languages. He learns them primarily while reading along the quays, or while threading his way through public squares while shadowing the serious auditors of the Sorbonne. At sixteen, he acts in the capacity of a professor of Hebrew and Sanskrit, which he performs with a certain success. I will allow myself to cite two students of the young professor: M. Michel Bréal, of the Institute, professor of the College of France, is his student in Hebrew; M. Paul Meyer, professor of the College of France, is his pupil in Sanskrit.[51] At eighteen, he becomes a tutor for the deaf-mute. He takes a course in chemistry and invents the phonograph, which he calls the paleophone. Then he begins to study medicine, practices it before becoming a doctor, and refuses to become one; he wants to remain a disheveled eccentric in science as in literature.

"I mentioned the phonograph earlier. Cros described the principle and construction of it in a sealed envelope, deposited at the

---

[51]Original footnote: This opinion by Alphonse Allais must be given tentatively.

Academy of Sciences, April 30, 1876. Not long afterwards, the *Semaine du clergé* (October 10, 1876), according to Charles Cros's instructions, confided to the Abbot Leblanc, gave a complete and perfect description of that instrument. Eight and a half months later, the American Edison takes out a patent, simply replacing a sheet of tin for Charles Cros's soot-coated glass.

"Charles Cros's scientific baggage is very considerable. I will merely cite his artificial production of amethysts, sapphires, rubies, topazes, etc. (crystallization and coloration of alumina), and his color photography, which will completely replace the old kind of photography. A study of the means of communication with the planets, wherein he claims that Mars and Venus have for a long time now been sending us signs that we don't understand. The *Mécanique cérébrale*,[52] a gigantic work presented to the Academy of Sciences, etc., etc."

It runs in the family. His family is essentially artistic and scientific. His father was a first-rate scholar, his brother Antoine Cros is a poet and physician, Henry Cros is a sculptor. To wrap up this too-serious and dry analysis, I would like to recount a legend that is current among the artist studios. Here it is.

The three Cros brothers come together one morning to lunch with their father. Antoine is more serious than usual and announces that at dessert he is going to make an important announcement. Between the pear and the cheese, the doctor Antoine, who is holding a small piece of paper in hand, proffers this: "My dear father, my dear brothers, I have finally discovered the means to make all men *immortal*. And I have the proof."

Immediately, Charles and Henry clap their hands: "Bravo! bravo! Finally!!!"

But the father remains quiet and gloomy; his face assumes an indescribable look of suffering.

"So, father?" asks Antoine.

At which point, the father rises and says: "What? you want to prolong, to eternalize this miserable, mean life, where injustices, poi-

---

[52]*Mécanique cérébrale:* cerebral mechanism or intellectual mechanics.

sons, physical and moral leprosies abound? You want to bind us forever to this base and backwards planet? You would want to deprive
us of the long-awaited heavens?... No, my son, you will not do that,
will you? No, I beg you..."

The three brothers were floored; then, suppliants, they cried:
"Let them, let men have immortality!!!"

The inflexible father declared: "I don't want it! no!!!"

Then, pale, Antoine throws into the fire the mysterious piece
of paper, while the brothers say: "Father, father, you are nothing but
a Saturnian, you devour your children!"

Such is the legend. The truth is that the three brothers, extraordinarily gifted, showed themselves from then on to be capable
of undertaking anything and succeeding at it, when constancy sus-
tained them in their efforts.

Perseverance, that bovine virtue, which permits one to continue to the end of the furrow, did not fall to the lot of Charles, a
winged being, culling a little dew here and a little honey there
among the flowers, without wishing to condense the juice usefully.
Great discoverer of ideas that others exploited, witness Edison.

He who had invented the monologue, that genre that had
such success, and continues to succeed so well, he complained – oh!
amicably, without any bitterness – that it was Coquelin cadet who
benefited by it rather than him.

The *Obsession*, the *Bilboquet*[53] (a pure masterpiece of veiled
irony) and so many other pieces that it would take too long to list
them all, delivered by the whimsical comedian, consecrated his repu-
tation at concerts and soirées. Naturally, Cadet gave the name of the
author; but what of it? the public exclaimed: "What wit! that Cadet!
what verve! where does he come up with all that?" Try and counter
that if you will. So much so however that Charles Cros remained
practically unknown, alone at his office or in his laboratory, at the
same time even when, in fashionable salons, his works enchanted audiences.

---

[53]Bilboquet: a cup and ball game.

One sad evening, quite a rare event for Charles, he expressed himself to me in these terms: "Neither glory, nor money, that's rough!"

So, from then on, I dug my heels in: I wanted to develop a system that would make poets speak their own works; to find a stage, whatever it might be, and put before the public the singers of rhyme, with their Normand or Gascon accent, with their incoherent gestures or awkward allures; but with that one very particular thing: that savor of the author bringing to light himself the expression of his thought.

From that time forward, I spoke about this thing. People objected to me that poets would lack as such a little of the pontifical dignity that one imposes on them in the name of I don't know what; besides, several of them felt too timid to declaim their poems to more than three or four people, and they still needed to have behind them the fireplace of a salon, or the corner of a piano, to give them countenance. I responded that the troubadours and the trouvères,[54] who were great in their time, mixed the art of speaking well with the art of thinking well and the art of expressing themselves well; that, moreover, the art of the comedian, after having been held in contempt for so long, had been acclaimed in the most straight-laced of settings, that they drew glory and money from the poets' verse, and that, my faith, the poets, without claiming the money, ought at least to recuperate the glory. I added that timidity is soon vanquished by the exercise, and I cited myself by way of example, me, who had been the most timid among provincial gazelles. They heard me out. I might add here that, since then, after some practice, that doctrine appeared solid, and that one or another poet whom I will not name here, and who claimed at that time that it was contrary to all professional dignity to declaim, himself, his modest rhymes before the crowd, has since then not hesitated to give conferences before a paying public, either in Paris, or Belgium, or Switzerland, trying, as much as possible, to attain the art of the comedian. If that was all the hydropaths produced, it would be something.

Moreover, that novel publicity seemed necessary in the years

---

[54]Troubadours... trouvères: medieval French singers, song-writers, and poets (poet-musicians), the former in *langue d'oc*, the latter in *langue d'oïl*.

1877-1878; because, at that time, the literary journals of the Latin Quarter or Montmartre were either dead or buried. Several collections alone, wherein the subscribers paid to have their own verse inserted, were limping along, while offering to insert the poem or photograph of the first-place laureate of a monthly contest for free. It was in this way that *le Parnasse*, by Georges Berry, was founded, who focused less on poetry at that time than on garbage collection, and never dreamed, I imagine, that one day he would become a municipal councillor of the good city of Paris.

That *Parnasse* however had the happy fortune of discovering a poet, Edmond Haraucourt, and a young literary hack, Émile Michelet, who concealed his name and went by the transparent pseudonym of Telehcim.

Georges Berry was bound moreover to found many other journals before finding his true path. These are those trials and errors of beginnings, those vagabondages through similar ideas, that I call the Bohemianism of the Spirit. One beats the bushes empty, until one finds finally the magpie in the nest, and then the Bohemian life becomes a dream of the past, and one is a *made man*.

For the wandering poet, the Latin Quarter seemed horribly deserted. No editorial offices, where one could hold forth wrongly or rightly; no more little cabarets, such as the *Sherry-Cobbler*. Alas! Joséphine had closed shop, because her leased ended, and she went one knows not where, to the Marais, it's said.

Sometimes, the illustrious Sapeck passed by rapidly, with André Gill, with whom he worked in order to become a profound caricaturist like his master. The poor master, whose mind later was to sink into madness, gave one the impression at that time of a French Musketeer: a large hat that the only thing it was missing was a panache – and still it seemed that that panache was there, standing up straight towards the sky or bending in the breeze, so much did that haughty head, the long hair, the turned-up mustache, give superb bearing to that headgear. Yes, the panache was there, we saw it, I swear, when André Gill passed by, ample, his chest pushed out, emphasizing with a great big or rounded gesture his pompous and embellished phrases. Yes, the Musketeer! Not at all perhaps by vocation of pride, nor by contempt for the rest of humanity. Certainly not:

those who knew him best have all declared that fundamentally Gill was a timid man. That timidity, he hid it under a great, affected eloquence. His pose – what the envious called his pose – was nothing but the effort of an enraged sheep. That gentle soul of an artist is dead because of that disparateness.

It suffices, to convince oneself of that duality that existed in Gill, to compare his monumental phrases, his strange rodomontades that have remained famous, and with which he stepped on his fellow citizens, with certain published poems from one day to next, and which were collected much later under the title of: *la Muse à Bibi.*

What is more intimately annoying and sweet than this piece: *le Chat botté?*[55]

> *Matou, charming, with his wild ideas,*
> *Cat, unique treasure of beggars,*
> *   Cat that one adores*
> *In ones infancy, and that, very old,*
> *   One still loves.*
>
> . . . .
> *Ah! how he was, my Puss in Boots,*
> *Gleaming with love and gaiety,*
> *   When, bold cat,*
> *With exorbitant attitudes,*
> *He preceded my sweet twenty*
> *   Crying: "Make way!*
> *Make way for the marquis de Carabas!*
> *Ohé! all of you, above, below,*
> *   Make way for my master!*
> *Admire, astonished people,*
> *The man, from the tip of his nose*
> *   To his gaiters,*
> *And start to proclaim, churls,*
> *That the woods, meadows, fields,*
> *   New flowers,*
> *Skies, from today on,*
> *Are his, his the laurels,*

---

[55]*Le Chat botté*: the Puss in Boots.

His the beauties!
If you should doubt unfortunately!
You would be – I wipe a tear away,
        When I think about it –
My word: the Puss in Boots,
Chopped into mincemeat,
        Chopped without respite!..."
Thus spoke, at that moment,
My cat in a party suit...

Goodbye, he added, melancholily, goodbye dreams!

"Pink horizons! green paths!
Chateaus in Spain! Baskets!
        The vendage is over!"

And here is the puss in boots, alas!

        ... finished, moldy,
Unshod forever, almost –
        Paralytic,
And I'm quite afraid at each moment
To see dying of exhaustion
        My childhood friend,
Whom, for less solemnity,
I here call the Puss in Boots,
But who is also called Hope.

While, weary from his supreme effort at the *Lune rousse*,[56] during the period of May 16, the caricaturist-poet sang so sadly about the passing of his dreams, he continued nonetheless bravely, blusteringly even, with a naïve braggadocio, to appear young yet in aspect, from Bullier to Élysée-Montmartre,[57] through crazy cabarets, through joyous nights, prolonging Hope even, pulling on the shagreen, and not willing yet to put away that tenacious Puss in Boots of

---

[56]*Lune rousse*: a satirical weekly founded by Gill (AD 1876-1879).

[57]Bullier... l'Élysée-Montmartre: two popular ballrooms of the time.

which he was the Marquis de Carabas.

And then there was a series of bizarre anecdotes, extravagantly heroic remarks, when the Count de Guinnes, hidden beneath the democrat André Gill, revealed himself to his stunned listeners.

One day, we were descending the rue Saint-Jacques as a group. A teasing comrade teased Gill, telling him that his fame and his popularity, which he believed to be so great amongst the people, did not extend beyond men of letters, artists, and politicians.

"We will see," said Gill. And, seeing a workshop where a cobbler was nailing some soles, he stopped and said to him:

"Do you know André Gill, you?"

The cobber stopped his work, and, after an instant of reflection.

"Gille!" he said with a strong accent, "Gille! No, there's no one by that name here."

"But André Gill, the caricaturist?"

"Caricaturisht!" said the other man; "I don't know him."

"Ah, well!" replied the illustrator, with a grand gesture, "eh well! you're the only one!"

At Bullier, which he frequented assiduously, Gill was sitting at a table in the company of some artists; a pretty girl joined them.

"Well, well, well!" said someone, "Pretty woman! Count yourself happy: this here is M. André Gill, whom you must know."

"Ah!" she said, "I believe I do, yes." And addressing herself to Gill: "You're the one with two brothers, pharmacy students."

"Two brothers!" Gill responded in his big bass voice, "Two brothers! I do have two brothers, but they are in marble, and standing on socles, at the Louvre!"

Anecdotes of this kind are legion in the great illustrator's biography. One of his friends, having returned to Paris recently from a trip to the Midi, paid him a visit:

"Eh," said the caricaturist, "where did you go, my dear friend?"

"To Nice."

"To Nice? What for?"

"Damn!" replied the other, "to bathe in the Mediterranean."

"You bathe! Me, when I want to wash, I go to the ocean: it's the only basin that suits me."

There was that discrepancy between the personal timidity of the dreamer and the pride of the public man which must have, over time, unhinged that brilliant mind. The megalomania slipped through the cracks and wrecked havoc, carrying with it the gentle poet and the grandiloquent tribune, the good boy of the suburbs and the man thirsting for millions.

I will have the occasion to speak of him again, in the context of the Hydropaths and the Chat Noir, where he brought the last glimmers of his wavering mind.

The relative solitude in which I found myself in that old Latin Quarter gave me the calm necessary to dig into my cartons and pull out, piece by piece, what equated to a volume of verse that I entitled *Fleurs du Bitume*.

Exiled for six years, far from fields, far from river banks, living exclusively in a banal room of a furnished hotel, or wandering through the streets, on the asphalt sidewalks and in the cafés, which served as covered prolongations of the sidewalk, I didn't have to compose my bouquet with any other flowers than those that pushed up from the asphalt: Vagabond poets, girls that strolled by, reveries under the gas lamps, like frail trees of light, public ballrooms, nocturnal restaurants. My wallet empty, my stomach even more so, my heart without love! And sometimes, by the chance windfall of some unexpected gain that allowed me to make up for it by a double portion of morsels and triple the kisses! The piggery of castaways on the *Vessel of Paris*, like the *Raft of the Medusa*; the unappeasable gluttony of Bedouins stumbling, after long days of fasting and thirst, onto some rich oasis of fruits that hunger renders extraordinarily savorous. Then the horrors of privation again! The solitary despairs! Those that one conceals from others and that are exhaled, at night, in the mansard, under the gaze of indifferent stars that turn slowly, far away, above the fanlights whose iron arm, perpetually extended, – the gallows at home – seems like an invitation to some definitive hanging; while a meager coke fire, reddening on the minuscule grill, gives suicidal ideas to the stove.

All that, I tried to capture it in the venomous and violent bouquet of the *Fleurs du Bitume*.

With the relentlessness of jailers, I was consoled by relentless work. And I enjoyed a relative peace, insofar as I hadn't written the phrase: The End.

But that fateful and joyous phrase, that phrase: *The End*, signified its opposite: The Beginning; the beginning of the runaround with publishers, potential patrons, influential masters. The *end* of the poet, the *beginning* of the traveling salesman, going door to door to offer his unsellable merchandise. The *end* of the work that carries with it its recompense and its joy, the *beginning* of martyrology. – Then, invincible timidity seized me again; it was all I could do to conceal that roll of paper under my overcoat, but it seemed to me that the piercing glances of passersby bore a hole through the fabric, tore off the cover, and had a field day with the rhymes; it seemed to me that, like wasps, the buzzing verses escaped from my pockets and enveloped me in a tumultuous swarm that had to attract the attention of little smiling female workers and mocking street urchins. I went along, head lowered in shame for being a budding poet, poor, dirty, opening an old umbrella riddled with holes, caught in a downpour that accompanies inevitably the unlucky.

One should smile when presenting himself to the amiable Parisians who are publishers; one should bear gloriously the dishonor of being young and unknown. On the contrary, with what terror one approaches the redoubtable fortress of books, how long one stands there spelling out the titles of the volumes put on display, the celebrated names appropriately placed on the yellow, red, blue, or green cover... The "to be or not to be" translated by: Shall I enter or shall I not?... Decided finally in any case, one enters, one has entered, it's the solemn moment; one tries to print on one's lips the smile of a friendly person, of a joyous Parisian, and it's a frightening rictus that is drawn there, writhing the mouth, while the eyes show alarm, and a sudden moisture develops on the forehead, and the temples contract... All those who have passed by there have more or less sensed the throes; but the poor fellow, isolated without anyone to vouch for him, barely trusting in his belief in himself, barely trusting in himself at all anymore even, looks silly, vague, lost in the publisher's antechamber. The worst poems of his collection, the most obscure phrases, the least well balanced, they dance in his head.

And according to the character, age, momentary mood of the publishing prince, the wretched candidate for glory receives an evasive or brutal, frank or dilatory response:

"Verse! verse!" says one. "Ah! no, no, no, not even if Homer signed it!"

"Write prose," says another.

A third looks the importunate fellow up and down scornfully:

"How's that! you, an unknown, you dare to present a volume? Make yourself known first."

"But," the applicant thinks, "if, to make oneself known, one must already be known, that's quite a paradoxical thing, unless one wishes to imitate Lacenaire, and to be known as an assassin before making a name for himself as a poet."

Others, finally, take the manuscript, keep it for three months without reading it, then give it back one fine morning just as they received it.

And throughout this crazy journey, one goes to request among the powerful, or those whom one believes as such, a letter for the publisher. It was in this way that I visited Barbey d'Aurévilly, and Émile Zola.

Barbey d'Aurévilly declared that I was an unbearable realist, while Émile Zola accused me of exaggerated Romanticism.

I quickly had had enough, of the judgment of masters.

The great literary jurors are nowise prophets in the realm of literature: it is their country after all.

Two and one half years were spent in this way.

Finally, the idea, that should have come to me at the very beginning, finished by hatching on my horizon, devastated of all other hopes: the publisher Lemerre!

The *Flowers of Bitumen*, after a favorable review by the reader at that time, M. Anatole France, the exquisite poet of *Noces corinthiennes*, today literary columnist at the *Temps*, was accepted and, despite a serious strike put on by the typographers, which devastated the printers of Paris at that time, was published in 1878.

Ed'io anché, me also, I could now stroll through the galleries of the Odeon, become popular at the Bullier ballroom, and believe on my star: I was in Elzevir[58] under a yellow jacket.

My colleagues at the ministry gazed at me with somewhat strong criticism in their eyes, and some even took advantage of my being a poet as demonstration to the bureau chief that I had no more need for advancement: they passed over me at the next promotion.

What did I care about bureaucracy. Now I had confidence – naïve, o naïve confidence! – My life was just beginning.

Illusions of a bachelor who believes that all his troubles lie behind him when everything is just beginning! But what joyous hours! First book! first love! The harshest criticisms at that time resembled a certification of glory!

One can certainly die of hunger a little to obtain that.

---

[58]Elzevir: a reference to the famous Dutch bookmaker/publisher of the 17th and 18th centuries.

Chapter Seven

*The musical inspiration. – The Besselièvre concert: Gungl's Hydropaten
waltz. – A tenacious nickname. – Canadian explication. – The Rive
Gauche. – October 5, 1878. – October 11, 1878. – The Hydropaths. –
The sessions. – The rage of drinkers. – The police: quarter eye and a
quarter ear. – M. Andrieux, prefect of police. – Women artists.*

For beings of imagination, music without words – symphony or
waltz, sonata or fanfare of horns – is the great and artificial manufacturer of dreams. The chance chords make one feel beautiful, rich,
glorious, loved. One hears a deep rumbling within himself, like
armed vehicles filled with rhymes, sonorous poems; or perhaps one
suffers, one groans, one grows emotional, one weeps, one feels his
soul get lost in the overly thick shadows or under the decidedly distant stars; and at the back of one's skull, like penitent phantoms,
strophes exit and slide in cadence; or maybe it's a flight, an orgiastic
whirlwind, kisses that one steals and cups one breaks, while the diverse timbers of the orchestra respond, striking chords like the feet
of ballerinas on an elastic parquet.

There was, on Sundays, for fifteen sous, the *paradise* of the
People's concert. One needed an *ad hoc* outfit: a soft hat and resis-
tant jacket. Because one fought for Wagner, in that *paradise*, and on
several occasions, under an avalanche of hissers, the applauder had
to go, head first, up the steep steps above the crania of the listeners.
All was not roses in that musical career. Happily, most of the time,
we, the applauders, we stayed together, and my faith! some hissers
got what they deserved.

Music for music! Ah! why did Wagner compose poems!
Why does one want to make us applaud him as a librettist? At the
end of the day, the music does not exist any less, right? But I prefer
the suggestions that it offered to me then to the legends it pretends to
impose on me today: *opera, non verba*, one could say with a Latin
play on words: *opera, not words.*

Sometimes, during the week, one went to the Besselièvre
concerts. There one found the minuet of the symphony in G minor

by Mozart, and also modern dances. Let's not speak badly about the waltz, okay?

One evening, I found myself with the Viscount Alfred de Puy... whom we called familiarly Puy-Puy and who resembled Henry IV as well as the Duke de Nemours; although aristocratic, he was a colleague of mine at the ministry of finance. We went to that Besselièvre concert together, and, filled with melancholy, I listened as the numbers of the program wound down, when all of a sudden a waltz with a crystalline rhythm struck me. It was as if drops of water had tintinnabulated on panes of glass, or better, as if one had made Champagne glasses ring by the aid of silver knives.

"Remarkable dance!" I cried out. I had to know its name.

The program was placarded in a wooden frame against a tree. I found the number, and I read: Gungl', *hydropathen-valsh*.

Hydropathen-valsh! German! *valsh* is sufficiently comprehensible even for the most diehard Latinist; but hydropathen? What was that *Valse des hydropathen*? I interrogated in vain the people I knew, no one could tell me. The following day, at the ministry, at the restaurant, in the cafés on the Left Bank, I trotted out my question: What is *hydropathen*? It was my "Have you read Baruch?" I did it so much and so often, bothering folk with that refrain, that they nicknamed me the *Hydropath*.

In the grand gallery of annuities, I bore that ridiculous title serenely, until the day when the false deaf man, that colleague vis-à-vis whom I had, previously, employed that invertebrate language, came and asked me – me, who did not know anything – an explanation of my pseudonym; for the nonce, I improvised a theory that stuck:

"Near the confines of the polar circle, in Canada, in Labrador, in Greenland, there exists a species of remarkable animals whose paws are made of crystal, in the form of Champagne flutes, ornamented by a round foot, similar almost to the rackets that indigenous hunters used to walk on fresh snow. Those animals are made of snow doubtless, and ice; their eyes resemble multicolor pearls. Moreover, as they dance in the moonlight, their crystal paws, striking each other, give to the rare voyageurs there the sensation of a concert where one might hear harmonicas only. Gungl' made something like this," I added, "by writing a tintinnabulating and strange waltz by the name of *Hydropathen-valsh*. Only, in his ignorance of the French language, he put an 'h' after the 't', in place of two 't's; for *hydro* would mean *water* (from the Greek word *udor*), water, rock crystal, and pathen means paw, from which *waltz of the paws made of crystal*. I took that name," I declared to the false deaf man, "because Nebuchadnezzar – O symbol! – possessed feet of clay; ourselves, humble democrats, we have feet of glass that death must break one day. And that's why I am *Hydropath* with an 'h' or Hydropatte with two 't's."

That illuminating explanation was accepted; and I continued, from the Bullier dance hall to the Louvre, through the cafés and the restaurants, to be denominated the *Hydropath*.

If I give such long explanations here, it is because many times, and even recently in the *The Searchers' Intermediary*, curious people have asked the reason for that bizarre title: Hydropath!

I will get on with my story then.

The need to recite verse and to sing songs made itself heard so much in that epoch that, little by little, a table d'hôte, located on rue des Boulangers, was transformed into a place of reunion. Richepin had passed by there, as well as Ponchon and Germain Nouveau; but nothing else remained scarcely save the Haitians who perpetually disputed the respective merits of Boisrond-Canal and Salomon, when Rollinat, having returned from the countryside, Georges Lorin, Sapeck, Léo Montancey, Baude de Maureceley, Puy-Puy and several others stopped by. A large garden adjoined the house, a room contained the indispensable piano and the indispensable armchairs. It was very gay: poetry, music, and dances reunited. Yes! There were even some high-society women who came... I will not say whom.

But the Haitians were determined to demand a little baccarat at the conclusion of those joyous reunions. And the accorded baccarat led to the inevitable police coming down on us, during the course of which, as I was fleeing through the gardens, I fell on the melon bells,[59] whose crystalline cracking sounds sounded less agreeable to my ears than Gungl's hydropathic and chromatic scales.

That place of reunion being closed, four or five of us settled on a small room, located on the first floor of the *Rive Gauche* café, at the corner of rue Cujas and boulevard Saint-Michel – today it is a bouillon shop. A hospitable piano welcomed us. But the door was, in accordance with the rules, open to all.

However, one evening – October 5, 1878 – it was that time of year when secondary school students were about to go back to school. A group of twenty young people, rather excited, descended on our place, and, in the last half hour of freedom remaining to them, they took possession of the piano and demandibulated three quarters of it, while shouting refrains, of which the most elegant was a song entitled *les Vidangeurs*:

> *Nothing need be lost,*
> *In nature, all is good,*
> *Squeeze, squeeze, the shoe on m...*
> *The morning shows on the horizon!*

That little session exasperated us. When the young vandals had up and left, we made the boss of the establishment come up, and we asked him under what conditions he would consent to hand over to us, for us and our friends alone, that small room equipped with a piano.

"If there are twenty of you," said that proprietor, "and you can guarantee consumption, it's a done deal; you choose what day of the week."

"Friday, for example!"

"Friday it is."

The five of us who were present at that historically memorable meeting were (in alphabetical order, so as to spare me any need to correct it): Abram, Émile Goudeau, Georges Lorin, Rives and Maurice Rollinat.

---

[59]melon bells: semi-spherical glass "bells" that are placed over melons to ripen them (much like greenhouses operate).

It was resolved that each of us would bring two, three, or four friends on the following Friday. The following Friday, we were seventy-five people in all. It makes one believe that the need to get together was cruelly felt. The assembly naturally overflowed from the small room into the large room with billiard tables and the adjoining rooms.

It was a beautiful session.

"When the French get together, they begin by electing a committee, then by trying to set up rules," said an illustrious traveler.

The assembly nominated Émile Goudeau president, with vice-presidents Georges Lorin and, on the refusal by Rollinat, M. de P..., the friend Puy-Puy, the Henry the IV with a monocle.

The president was of the opinion that for now all other formalities were terminated, and that one should begin, like good young men, to sing, drink, recite poetry, play the violin, pluck the guitar or monologue, ultimately abandon ourselves to all the frolics that the muses authorized.

Ah! yes siree! we needed to give a name to that assembly that, all of a sudden, was becoming a *Society*.

What would we call the *Society*?

Some proposed: *La Pipe en terre, les Escholiers, le Gay-sçavoir, les Fils de France*, long story short, all sorts of serious names borrowed from the repertory, and destined to indicate that one would be bored to death...

As president, I took advantage of my new situation, and, without telling anyone a thing, I made the vote be for the *Hydropaths*, on the pretext that it was a nickname that had been bestowed on me, that it weighed on me, and that I was planning to share it with others. I explained finally the origin of the word, and I insisted on the point, that, not having any common program, we should possess an original name that would not compromise the future doctrines of the Society, nor its possible apostasies.

And that's how, one Friday in October, the Society of the Hydropaths was founded. Several recalcitrants immediately called for a constitution, or at minimum a set of rules; but the majority, more practical, asked that the poets present should make themselves heard, as well as the musicians and actors. A sort of concert was improvised, bocks were passed round, and, towards midnight, at the word: "Time's up, until next Friday!" everyone went their separate ways.

This occurred on Friday, October 11, '78.

One has to believe that this type of distraction was extremely necessary for the young students of that distant past; because, the following Friday, more than one hundred people showed up, the majority of them forced to hang out in the hallways. In spite of that, the president easily obtained silence – O miracle!

But, on the third reunion, one hundred fifty people were jostling each other in that narrow space, and it was necessary to review the situation.

Swift emissaries, men of light feet, and voluntary reporters, had already discovered, at number 19 rue Cujas, a hotel whose vast rez-de-chaussée could be, at the close of the evening meal, transformed into a concert hall or even a dance hall.

By raised hands, we adopted that locale, and by raised feet we brought ourselves there, single file, in a flash.

A decision! a decision! Parliamentarism didn't exist at all yet at the Hydropaths. It was the heroic epoch when chiefs recently carried on the shield, chiefs with long hair and beards, knew how to make themselves understood by their warriors.

The policemen, surprised, saw the smiling hydropaths, – oh! smiling a little too much, that's all – and humming – oh! humming until they were out of breath – disappear into the mysterious Cujas hotel. And... they made a report to their chiefs.

But let's not get ahead of ourselves. That no bad feelings might affect the historian's quill! Let's be gay rather, even when trembling before the law: Tradéridéra!

The Hydropaths were made up of, at the beginning, an inextricable hotchpotch of diverse, contrary tendencies: think bouillabaisse. There were young politicians who dreamed of transforming the reunion into secret meetings, modernist poets who barely got along with the Romantics, amateurs who hazarded songs that were more than risqué or ultra-crusty monologues; people behind the times who dared to utter *Page, écuyer et capitaine*; young actors or students from the Conservatory who came to try their hand at reciting Théramène; while others, more adroit and with better taste, delivered Coppée's *la Bénédiction* or *la Grève des forgerons;* those out of their minds, mistaking the réunion for a café-concerthall, demanded brass bands; while others still, magisterially pontifical, didn't understand how one could laugh even once; the hullabalooers let out their balderdashes, and, next to them, certain elegiac Catholics dispensed hymns to the Virgin. There were even the obstinate and old nutcases who braved ridicule to climb up on the stage, like that old failure of an actor, not defatigable, who sang Victor Hugo's *Sarah* with a strong Italian accent, like this:

> *Sarah bello d'indoulenço*
> *Sou balanço*
> *Dans oun hamac, au-dessou*
> *Dou bassin d'ouné fontaino*
> *Touto pleino*
> *D'eau pouïsée à l'Illyssous.*

Naturally, there were students of law, medicine, pharmacy, but also those from the School of Fine Arts and from the Conservatory, ministerial or city hall employees, engineers and the sons of concierges, and even a certain number of simple drunks, come there to make some racket. It was a Chamber of Deputies in miniature: all ideal or real diversities jostled each other in that microcosm. And all that turned, swirled, simmered in its juice, seethed, frothed, made the lid jump and shook the pot to the point that the president, head chef, removed his apron and sent it to the devil. Fortunately, it was youth and laughter that took the upper hand. A group of *fumists*, taken with art, but cocky, banded together at that moment, saved the institution from the start, then, later, by the nature of things, brought it to ruin. There were also the peaceful spectators, like Bourget, Coppée, Monselet, Paul Arène, and others.

What follows will give an idea, more or less, of how things

transpired.

The president, Émile Goudeau, and the vice-president, A. de P***, whom we called Puy-Puy, set themselves up in the office. The office was located in a corner, from which one could see into both rooms, the which were furnished with chairs, tables, small round tables destined to receive the Chartreuses, mazagrans, and numerous bocks of the evening. When the two rooms were filled, the stewards went from row to row collecting the names of those in the crowd who desired to vibrate on the stage (a simple rug that stage!) or to launch some sharps and flats, to deliver some sonatas on the piano, or to make a violin or violoncello groan. The names were brought back to the office, and the president or his vice-president composed a list of acts, intercalating music and verse, and, as much as possible, the happy with the sad. While this operation was going on, a lively conversation was struck up, sometimes a simple murmur of noise, sometimes a cyclone. Little did it matter! But the little bell of the president rang suddenly; silence was re-established, and one after the other the poets, monologists, actors or singers, pianists or violinists, got on stage.

The thing, thus presented, gives the impression of having an august simplicity to it. Alas! alas! it was hardly a piece of cake.

The musicians wanted to monopolize the attention, while the disheveled and trepidatious poets barely put up with the chromatic, sometimes encumbering scales; the gay monologists couldn't stand the vague poets, historiated in the disparate groups; while the politicians of the assembly were right indignant that the rights of man were not discussed; the patriots had something against the German sonata, and the exasperated pianists would have gladly devoured two or three patriots. The *fumists*, having the redoubtable Sapeck at their head, thought of nothing but making fun of everything, while the convinced hierarchs pressured the presidential office to hold the banner of art high and firm. There was a series of internal conflicts that the simple public got caught up in. There was already the question of women: should young women be allowed in, married for fifteen days or fifteen hours to members of the Society? The pudibund and austere ephebes were down on women. On top of all that, the drunks, who had sometimes come on an empty stomach, prided themselves on an imaginary right to interrupt burlesquely the peaceful concerts of the Hydropaths.

The president, backed up fortunately by the founders, armed himself against the various pretensions, granting to everyone the right to leave if boredom took them. This reasoning was generally accepted by the majority who voted by raised hands in favor of his office. But the politicians were wily: attributing to the Parliament the most reprehensible practices, oftentimes an interpellator would stand up, formulating a long series of amendments to a rule that didn't exist. That raised tempests and hailstorms; but, ruthless, the president argued that the Society, being literary and artistic, accepted the politicians as possible men of fine words, but never as directors.

One day, put on the hot seat, the president turned in his resignation – O shadow of M. Thiers! – That redounded perfectly to his credit, and he was reinstated, immediately. Since then, the beaten politicians acquiesced, content to come together as they wished, in the shadow of literature, fine arts, and the perpetual piano.

The drunks were less accommodating. One evening of dissertation, a procession of young men arrived whose festoons worried the glasses. A festoon is nothing; but bizarre cries left their chests, lit up like forges by the imitation champagne of modest restaurants. From then on, a trouble difficult to put down and constantly rising up again. The poet on stage, or the violoncellist, exasperated, stopped in mid-phrase and withdrew, bitter, saying: "Those miserable wretches prevent me from continuing!"

Many a tumult ensued. Finally, an order of business, energetically voted for by the assembly, authorized the president to transform into a gendarme under such circumstances, alas! frequent enough, and to throw out the delinquents.

That operation presented difficulties often enough. The inextricable brawls, that seemed drawn by Gustave Doré, transformed the place into the scenes of a battlefield, while the peaceable folk, and the energetic women, climbing up on their chairs, against the walls, watched the terrible and fuliginous melee. Thanks to several giants, and also the virtue in numbers, the *lit* were put outside. Most of the time, they left vociferating, then, eight days later, very calm, they effected their return, with the smiling good-naturedness that presides over that sort of remorse.

Sometimes however some of them were more fierce. In the beginning, one of those types, expelled by a giant, waited for me by the door, with the tenacity of ivy, and said to me:

"You will hear from me tomorrow morning."

Then he disappeared, a zigzagging shadow, enormous in the fog.

I have to say that on exit from the sessions, the literary celebrations, deemed diurnal until fifteen minutes to midnight, became essentially nocturnal until morning. I returned home then at the sound of the cock – because, rue Monsieur-le-Prince, where I inhabited the hotel (furnished, alas! yes), possessed a certain number of coalmen and churls who raised hens, in the street, if you please, and for whom the males, in the dust at the back of a dark shop, made vigorous appeals, at the crack of dawn. A Saint Peter of goodwill would have been able to hear then, not only three times, but thirty times three the matutinal clarion of remorse. The Saint Peters of noctambulism, bowing their head at the sound, were returning home. Oh! to sleep finally!

I was soon woken by a discrete but clear knock-knock.

"Come in," I said, "the key is in the hole!"

O candor of anticapitalists! Suave security of *omnia-mecum-porto* nice guys, son of the philosopher Bias!

Two young men, each wearing a frock coat buttoned up to his neck, made their entry. I mistook them at first for bailiffs – So young!! – No, they were witnesses for the... drinker, expelled the night before.

They explained themselves. As soon as I understood, I asked them to turn around towards the wall, seated on some chair, to allow me, in my single reception room-bedroom, to get myself into a state suitable to receive them.

When I was done, I said to them:

"You can turn around now and speak with me."

As soon as they explained to me that their client, seriously insulted by me the other night, and put outside a *club* (sic) by my henchmen, demanded reparation by a duel, I reflected: "My faith! it's such superb weather! instead of going to the languishing office, it would not be unpleasant to climb some hill, and lie down on the grass."

"Yes! but after that first battle, how many others? All the delicious drinkers and quarrelers of the Latin Quarter would take care not to miss out on so good a windfall!"

Then, as serious as Molière's Master Jacques, I responded to the two witnesses:

"It is to Émile Goudeau himself, employee of the ministry of finance, and sometime poet, or to the president of the Hydropaths that you address yourselves?"

They consulted between themselves for a moment, then responded:

"It is to the president of the Hydropaths."

"Ah, well!" I replied, "since yesterday evening, a quarter to midnight, one minute after the session was over, I ceased to be president of the Hydropaths until next Friday, nine o'clock in the evening, when I will say: 'Session is open!' Until that time, I am nothing but a simple citizen, having no authority over anything whatsoever, and by consequence no responsibility to incur."

A faint smile appeared on their lips:

"Then," they say, "you refuse reparation, and we can proceed with legal proceedings."

"Perfectly," I responded energetically; "the president of the Hydropaths, having had an obligation to maintain order, which care was confided in him, did not hesitate to put out of doors your client; it is in the capacity of president that he acted, and he is prepared to receive a complaint, at the next assembly, and, if he has abused his power, to be held accountable or make excuses."

The young men smiled more and more.

"But," I added, "if your client has a bone to pick with me personally, I can be found, at 5 pm, at such and such café, on the terrace; he will need only to shake my table while passing, or turn over my glass, to see that I know how to respond to him. I want only my personal quarrels; but as president, I'm merely a bell, and a call to order."

They departed, satisfied. In this way, I avoided all confusion between my ordinary role as a *bon vivant*, and what the discipline necessary in a tumultuous assembly imposed on me in an abrupt, sometimes brutal, but absolutely necessary fashion. Those who attempted to preside after me became fully aware of those little solemnities. What was needed, in that Latin Quarter, amongst the young men fresh out of their voluntary service of one year, was a sergeant's grip, but, on top of that, a great deal of diplomatic velour, and the frank laughter of a comrade.

If it sounds like I'm pleading *pro domo*, too bad, but I continue.

Diplomacy? A great deal more of it was needed with respect to the laws of the land, the magistrature, and the police. With the gatherings becoming enormous, three hundred fifty people piling into a moderately-sized space, invading the hallways and the kitchen of the hotel, the gigantic programs, whose numbers succeeded one another as rapidly as possible, could not be gotten through in one night, so we had two sessions a week, Wednesdays and Saturdays. But the police, who had already been keeping an eye, or a quarter of one, on our Friday-night sessions, began to gnash their teeth when the number doubled: that made, in their eyes, six hundred conspirators, accompanied by various women, who swarmed 19 rue Cujas, for unknown reasons. Through closed shutters, the quarters of an eye cast sidelong glances, and took in the exasperated gestures of Paul Mounet as he recited *la Grève des Forgerons*, or Maurice Rollinat's convulsions as he spoke *la Soliloque de Troppmann*, or Coquelin Cadet's surprising expressions, or André Gill's bristling mustache, and sometimes the president even as he violently raised his voice, whose hair stood on end, while his hand energetically shook a handbell for public order, a real bell.

"All that is not natural!" thought the quarter glances. "There are women, perhaps it's a group of nihilists."

One spoke a lot about skepsis in those days, skepsis, not men, not women, who conspired without determinate gender.

When the constables saw some giants throw recalcitrant drinkers outside, they thought it must be the execution of a traitor, and they greeted the expelled person at the exit.

"What are people doing inside?" they asked.

"They're vile churls! a bunch of poets and pianists! they can go to hell with their Baudelaire! and down with their Wagner!"

That's all that the quarter ears could extract from the banished, who went away to other regions, without treason.

To the point! one evening of the Hydropaths, while – I remember it well – Monselet, Coppée, Bourget, Paul Arène, and others, very grave, attended the session, the boy came to warn me in a low voice that the owner of the hotel was asking for me, now, oh! but now. I ceded the presidency to Puy. And I went.

In the hotel office, the owner, pale and desperate, was arguing with four keepers of the peace and a police sergeant.

"Ah!" he said on seeing me, "here he is: M. the President."

"So you're the president," said the police sergeant to me brusquely.

"I confess," I said humbly.

Seeing me so humble, he continued:

"Then, you have a permit to reunite people here."

"No," I said, even more humbly.

"Eh, well," said the police sergeant resolutely, "we're going to make you evacuate the premises, given you don't have the right to hold a public gathering here, and you do it twice a week."

I grew cocky, and taking the police sergeant by the arm, I led him, him and his men, to the glass door, which gave onto the session room; the inside curtain having been half-raised, they could cast a glance around.

"Do you see," I said to them, "that large gentleman (it was Villain) over there, well, he's an actor with the Théâtre-Français, and he recites Victor Hugo's verse. You see those young men and those young women, they are calm; wait, they are applauding..."

"It is true that it's like at the theater," said the police sergeant. "But we are obliged to run you out, all the same..."

"Well," I said, "I will go back, sit down at my desk, and announce your invasion. Keep in mind that I will not say a thing, and that those people there who are so calm will be much less so in a moment. As for me, you will be obliged to tear me from my office, and I will cry like an eagle, and roll on the floor..."

"So you will rebel," responded the police sergeant severely.

"Me, not yet. Listen: how about this! File a complaint against me; tomorrow, I will pay a visit to the captain of police, and, in this way, you will spare you and your men the trouble of chasing out three hundred people, who will not go easily."

They filed a complaint against me, as well as the hotel owner.

The following morning, at nine o'clock, I presented myself before the captain of police. That magistrate, contrary to my expectation, I must say, showed himself to be quite friendly.

"Yes," he said, "I had given the order, but just last night, my son, who is a student, found himself in attendance and was charmed. And that's that! but submit an application as per the rules, I will support it, and from then on, promise me that you will maintain internal order."

And me, parodying Napoleon III:

"Order? I guarantee it!"

That occurred while M. Gigot was prefect of police.

Several days later, I found myself, at the *Marmite Républicaine* banquet – a gathering of senators, deputies, politicians, and artists – next to M. Andrieux who announced, from that moment forward, his candidacy to the Prefecture of police. As I was narrating to him that skirmish, he said to me:

"My god! the police want to place their hands on you; do you think they are going to let you, you and your friends, handle three or four hundred young men? All the same, insist on it, and the case will be decided in your favor. If you had asked in advance, you would have been denied; but, after the fact, you have a chance."

When M. Andrieux replaced M. Gigot, some time later, I recalled to him our conversation, and he recommended me to the head of the third bureau of police, who was in charge of concerts, artistic gatherings, etc., etc.

There, I had to furnish some statutes. I improvised five articles at a café table. The bureau chief pointed out to me that I was missing an *indispensable* article: women were not allowed at the sessions.

What the hell! What the devil! and all the audience at the Hydropath's, or almost all, came there only because they were just about married.

"But," I blurted out to the bureau chief, "what if Mme. Sarah Bernhardt, who was happy to accept the title of Hydropath,[60] deigns to attend one of our sessions and makes her golden voice be heard?"

"Oh! Mme. Sarah Bernhardt," said the chief, "by god! She's not a woman, she's a great artist..."

"Good," I responded, "but if such and such other actress, Mlle. Réjane, or Mlle. Reichemberg, wanted to come, must we shut the door in their face?..."

"No, no, of course not, they are actresses..."

"But... the students at the Conservatory?"

"Fine, fine, fine, they are destined for dramatic careers..."

---

[60]Original footnote: it's true.

"But... but... the young women who are preparing later on to enter the Conservatory..."

"Enough! enough!" cried the chief, "you are a right jolly practical jokester. Let's finish up: you will receive, under your care, and on account of our tolerance, all the women you want; but so that we retain the right to revoke the permission in the event of scandals, you will add that article: 'women are not permitted to the sessions of the Hydropaths.'"

So it was added. And the women came, and the rhymes were sometimes interspersed with flirtations, – oh! discreet! as a result of that famous comminatory article; nevertheless, we did not overdo it except on exit, under the pale light of the moon, and under the paternal eyes of the absent policemen.

Chapter Eight

The Hydropath *sessions. – Performing poets. – Young actors. – Quasi Homeric numbers. – For me the phonebook! – Hydropathic songs. – Popular songs. – Let's proclaim the principles of art!*

I would like to give an impression of those extraordinary sessions, sometimes tumultuous for no reason at all, but most often peaceable, as the beloved authors and speakers appeared on stage... (because there was a stage, rue de Jussieu, and place Saint-Michel, no. 1). I don't want to bore the reader by being as thorough as possible. Many young people stopped by, whose names might escape me today; but nobody can be made accountable to the impossible. The *Hydropaths* was not a little church, but a sort of *forum* open to everyone; from then on, the census was nearly impossible. I will cite then randomly and impartially, as if, elected president again, I had to organize a Hydropathic session. – O old curule seat, presidential pipe, and bocks of honor! Heavens! it's nice to be young!

Census! census! It was Maurice Rollinat who had just declaimed, in his loud voice filled with lamentation, Dupont's *les Platanes* which he had written the music to, and who, with his hair flopping in his face, darting terrible glances, and writhing his mouth into a Satanic rictus, uttered the terrible *Troppman's Soliloquy*, or one of his other pieces: *Mademoiselle Skeleton*, *The Wax Woman*, etc.[61] Author, actor, composer, singer, and pianist, Maurice Rollinat achieved an incredible success. If I had only to cite the pieces, or music, that made the Hydropaths stamp their feet in approval, in a delirium of applause, I would be obliged to draw the list from those poems, *The Heathlands* and *The Neuroses*, and from his songs published by Hartman. Anyone who has read them, but not heard him perform in person, has not known that marvelous artist at all.

It was Paul Mounet who, with a metallic voice, recited Victor Hugo's *Conscience* or Murger's *Testament*. Sometimes, disguising himself as a laborer, rolling up his sleeves on his large biceps, pass-

---

[61]Original footnote: *The Heathlands, The Neuroses* by Maurice Rollinat, Charpentier publisher.

ing a red scarf around his thick neck, and wearing a loose, blue blouse on his back, he played *la Grève des Forgerons*. It was Villain[62] who recited the *Ballad to the Moon*, by André Gill:

> *Bonnie blood of a bonnie God, make a wind,*
> *I put one foot in front of the other;*
> *But I'll never arrive at Montrouge.*
> *That's where I drank; no, I've drunk nothing;*
> *And to start with, I'm forbidden*
> *Unless it's with Alphonse Lerouge.*

There was Leloir[63] who had just sung in a falsetto voice the old and so charming song, written by Émile Pessard, with words attributed to Mlle. de Longueville:

> *Sure as I live, one day last month,*
> *A quite marvelous thing happened to me;*
> *All alone I was, at the edge of a wood,*
> *My lover came to me, fresher than roses;*
> *He kissed me, a kiss that was sweet and sage,*
> *And then bitter, he did more bitter things still,*
> *So I said to him, growing angry:*
> *"Hold your tongue, I'll call my mother."*

> * * * *
> * * * *

> *Sure as I live, what happened to me then was*
> *Something new which I was not made for.*
> *And almost dead, a kiss did me in,*
> *That made me close my eyes, and be mute;*
> *I woke, but an awakening so sweet*
> *That I died again, so dear it was to me,*
> *So I said to him, without growing angry:*
> *"Hold your tongue, I'll call my mother!"*

There was Coquelin Cadet from whom three or four mono-

---

[62]Original footnote: Of the Comédie-Française.

[63]Original footnote: At that time, of the third Théâtre-Français (the old Déjazet), later of the Comédie-Française.

logues were requested, and, to finish off, *le Hareng saur*, by Charles Cros.

> *There was a large wall, bare, bare, bare,*
>   * * * *
> *I have told this story, simple, simple, simple,*
> *To annoy some fellows grave, grave, grave,*
> *And to amuse the children small, small, small.*

And the grown-up children were amused also.

There was Charles Cros himself who came, with his bizarre behavior, his troubled air, forgetting those crazy subjects of laughter, which is usual for him, while dreaming about so many defunct loves and so many, sometimes bitter, ironies of fate:

> *In your hair, brown wave that submerges the comb,*
> *On your quivering breasts, amber toned, bathed*
> *In the odor of dead sea wrack amidst stones, in the evening,*
> *I want to drop, drop by drop, vertiginous*
> *Essences – and, cold curls, gold Oriental*
> *Patiences[64] in bloom, on black tulle.*

> *Tearing open the packages from the land of pestilence,*
> *I will find, embroidered treasure, beaded, the jacket*
> *That poorly hides your breast and lets resplend, naked,*
> *Your flanks. And on your fingers I will slip rings*
> *Where beneath the sapphire, beneath the opal with indistinct*
>   *[glimmers,*
> *Sleep ancient fish with unknown effects.*

> *In the opium of your arms, in the hashish of your nape,*
> *I want to sleep despite the cries of an emasculated world,*
> *And the dagger that wants to pin us heart against heart,*
> *That between your breasts, making strange shift,*
> *Your blood of a woman in my blood of a man mixed,*
> *And Death will yield before the vanquisher Love.*

Or there was André Gill, who, with his booming voice, his

---

[64]Patiences: garden patience, yellow or curled dock, or *Rumex crispus*.

turned-up mustache, and disheveled hair, uttered the following:

HOROSCOPE

In spite of your mother's tears,
Ardent young man, you want it,
Your heart is young, your arms nervous,
Come fight against the chimera.

Use your life, use your vows
In ephemeral enthusiasm,
Drink to the bitter lees,
See your hair grow white.

Isolated, fight! Suffer! Think!
Fate preserves you in recompense
The disdain of a triumphant fool,

The august beard of apostles,
With pure heart and the eyes of a child
To smile at others' children.

Isn't it disturbing, in a flashback, to see that athlete, bellowing that "horoscope," him, who later would be hunched up under Charenton's terrible showers.

There was Charles Frémine, the coarse Norman boy, the minstrel of *Floréal*, the poet of *Pommiers*. There were Paul Arène, Buffenoir, Léon Valade. And Monselet reciting the famous sonnet about the pig:

I adore you, o pig, dear angel!

There was Georges Gourdon, a little too much taken with politics, and Melandir, the photographer, poet and dramaturge; Alphonse Laffitte, a happy fellow, Raoul Fauvel, a sad one; Adolph Martin, who was able to find for a famous word ending in -*erde* a very unexpected rhyme. An old *Incedible*[65] recounts the Battle of Waterloo, and terminates a little later thus, suppressing the "r":

---

[65]*Incedible*: the Incredibles (but without the "r" on purpose) or *Incoyables,* a kind of faddish subculture in Paris (AD 1795-1799).

When the English c'ied: Help!
Cambonne 'eponded to them: C'ap![66]

There was the poet Paul Marrot,[67] small, alert, and fearful of currents of air: he recited philosophical poems or gay pieces. *Les Tambours, la Bourse, les Larmes, les Assiettes peintes, la Tête du moine* (that I regret I am unable to cite). Here's a *street painting*:

I saw, crawling on the pavement,
A lamentable legless cripple;
He was tall like a table,
Sad like a slashed drum.

At his side, his thin woman
Asking for handouts,
And extracting languishing sounds
From the bowels of a shrill violin.

The cripple caused pity,
His state, which brought me to tears,
Added I don't know what charms
To his better half's violin.

Human race, ironic race,
To shake off your stoutness,
Poverty is not enough,
One needs a little music.

And Edmond Haraucourt, the poet with two faces, Sire de Chambley for offhand things, Haraucourt for serious. The author of *Naked Soul* and *Friends*:[68]

THE SHIELD

A woman's belly is like a shield
Cut from luminous and immaculate metal,

---

[66]C'ap: Crap in English for "M'ede" (or *Merde*") in French.

[67]Original footnote: Published by Lemerre.

[68]Original footnote: Publisher Charpentier.

Whose paleness bulges and curves down
       Towards a shadow where its point is hidden.

From the dark golden angle to the base of her naked breasts,
It is exposed, vaulting its round and full curvature;
And the majestic arc of its carnal edges
       Gleams in the furrows of her groin.

Meanwhile, chiseled on the moving escutcheon
Where the source and seeds of the world are sheltered,
Her navel resplends like a lively sun,
       A lively sun of blonde flesh!

– Magic shield that I cover my heart with!
Venus' aegis, o ivory Gorgon,
Whose joyous splendor blinds my rancor
       And shines during my black nights!

Medusa who chases from my saddened heart
The dragon of Boredom, which doesn't let me go;
Weapon of patience with which I have fought
       Against all disgusts in life!

I love you with a fanatic and grievous love;
For my only true moments of forgetfulness were born of lust,
And I slept on you like a dying soldier
       Who no longer counts his wounds.

That's why my grief has raised altars to you
In the deserted temples of my darkened heart;
And I come there to worship the immortal charms
       Of your consoling harmony.

And the Belgian poet Georges Rodenbach, whom a critic called the Coppée of Belgium, recited several pieces from his first volume: *Sadnesses.*[69]

Me who's always dreaming, me who never laughed,

---

[69]Original footnote: *Sadnesses*, publisher Lemerre.

I cannot resist a love that obsesses.
I must open my heart finally and cede,
And I offer my gaunt profile to kisses.

The study that my ideal dream is nourished on,
In the drama of days, is but a sad interlude;
It is love, love alone that will be the remedy,
For life is a tomb where love has flourished!...

I will give myself over to the instinct that carries me,
And – even if my heart should bleed! – I will open the door,
But you, unknown and indistinct woman whom I wait for,

Entering, remember that this heart is a total virgin,
That it is a temple full of brilliant dreams,
And don't behave as if you were in an inn.

There was Fernand Icres who asked Lebargy to read the following piece:

THE PACT
– For Émile Goudeau

One evening, Faust, abandoning grimoirs and retorts,
Listened to the cold winds moaning over the forest;
He watched the white shrouds of the clouds disappear,
And, noticing the great sky was empty, he despaired.

Then, suddenly, voices, he didn't know whence,
Like the shrill cries of a wolf that howled,
Cast, on every side of him, unknown notes...
The room lights up and Satan appears.

Satan! when, to the old atheist's somber call,
You came, you saw his blood-dipped quill
Trembling in the frightened hand that hesitated.

Well! as for me, for one night of love and delirium,
Mephisto! hand me the fatal parchment,

I will sign it without shuddering, – and without reading it.

Icres, a friend, a pupil of Léon Cladel, warmed up like that. Then, when he had composed *l'Ancienne, le Mitron,* etc., etc., he ran the risk of reciting them himself, which was after all the purpose of the Hydropaths.

Félix Décori, with his brother Louis Décori, who became an actor, and who played the role of *Marie-Pierre* so naturally in Richepin's *The Glue,* played Don Salluste and Don Cesar de Bazan in *Ruy-Blas,*[70] he also produced sonnets upon sonnets and ballads. I don't cite anything here. Félix Décori is today one of the best young assizes lawyers around. Perhaps he has forgotten about that pretty little thing that Fragerolle put, delicately, a touch of sentimental music to:

> *Margot! flourishing cheeks, perfumed lips,*
> *Smiled at the sweet speech of a squire-coxcomb.*

Now he booms: "Gentlemen of the Court, gentlemen of the jury. This is a social victim who...." He must miss Margot sometimes, us too... unless – yes! a sonnet is so quickly executed between two speeches for the defense.

There was Félicien Champsaur, who, with sober gestures, in a completely soft voice, murmured:

> *When she whom he loved, after having suffered*
> *For six months, without complaining, died quietly*
> *As April dies, and May, – he shut his door*
> *And went back to bed, for no reason and speechless.*
>
> *Sensing implacable laws weighing on him,*
> *He shed not a tear, but, a strange sort of dreamer,*
> *Near the white cadaver ready to be carried away,*
> *He wrote verses, his eyes fixed on her sometimes.*
>
> *In those verses, he put his soul, his very being;*
> *For the woman he adored, he wrote a long, sorrowful,*

---

[70] *Ruys-Blas:* a drama by Victor Hugo.

And poignant poem, a world... a universe...

It was a pure masterpiece, an immortal elegy;
In the open casket, silently he placed his verses,
So that no one else could read them but her.

And many other sonnets: *The Violets* (so pretty and Parisian!); *The Dragonfly*, etc., etc.[71]

Champsaur did better than just recite verse before the *Hydropaths,* he wrote a front-page article about them for the *Figaro*. His insertion in the *Figaro* garnered him moreover a duel, in which he wounded his adversary, but, in compensation, the journalist killed the poet by a fatal blow;[72] it is true that, from the ashes, Champsaur rose up as a novelist, the author of *Miss America*, a Parisian study, and *Coeur* along with many others, et cœtera.

And Jean Floux, whose volume of very Parisian verse is hard to find, and Théodore Massiac whose book, in manuscript, awaits a printer, and Gaston Sénéchal, whose bizarre fate reduced him to rendering counsel in the prefecture in Yonne, and Guy Tomel, who recited an archaic tale, *les Veilleuses du Paradis*, and Victor Zay who died so young, and Léo Trézenick who uttered *Gouailleuses*, and Charles Lomon, the author of *Jean d'Acier*, enacted at the Théâtre-Français, and Louis Tiercelin, and Armand Masson, and Joseph Gayda, the blond Meridional, who had less of an accent than Fernand Icrès, but who recited his *Volume* of verse slowly, and Eugène Godin, the author of *Cités noires*, and Mac-Nab, and Georges Lefebvre, who put on *la Cruche cassée* at the Taitbout theater and recited so amusingly *les Grenouilles qui*, and so many others... – to list them all would require the special talent of Homer. And Homer slept sometimes.

---

[71]Original footnote: published by Lemerre.

[72]The journalist mentioned here is Charles Vignier. He killed the poet Robert Caze in a duel that Caze had challenged him to... after a series of events stemming from the article that Champsaur had published. See Chapter LIX of Léon Bloy's *The Desperate Man*, in which Marchenoir, the main character (and a thin veil for Bloy) says this of Champsaur: "He is the only man of letters having dared to publish a book that plagiarized everyone...."

Then there is this, however, rising up from my memory, Guilleminot, a bard in eyeglasses, almost blind, half deaf, and an idealist, who declaimed, amidst shrill and misplaced laughter, fragments from Vercingétorix;[73] he had his success however with a small piece whose stanzas terminated with this refrain:

> *When you pass along the rutted path,*
> *Married couples, keep watch o' your horns,*
> *There's a howling wind a blowin'.*[74]

I must however reserve a place of honor for those who were vice-presidents, from the beginning, like Georges Lorin, and a little later, Georges Moynet and Grenet-Dancourt.

Lorin seldom presided, as he didn't like exercising authority (although it was necessary); he preferred to sketch *faces*, or chisel monologues in verse. They are his Parisian promenades: *les Maisons, les Gens, les Affiches, les Dames, la Ronde* (a little masterpiece), *les Ombrelles, les Éventails, les Voitures, les Arbres*, and many others et cœtera, which were collected later in a volume of verse entitled, *Paris-Rose*,[75] illustrated by Cabriol and Luigi Loir. One had to hear Lorin recite these lines in a faraway, snowy tone of voice:

> *Their eyes straight ahead, lined up*
> *Like soldiers in battle,*
> *The houses in cut stone,*
> *Watching waves upon waves*
> *Of Parisians, strangers,*
> *Running, amidst the dangers*
> *Of treacherous sidewalks and carriages,*
> *After gold and adventures,*
> *With heavy or light steps.*

---

[73]Vercingétorix: (82-46 BC) king of the Arverni, a Gaulic people, defeated by Julius Caesar, and kept later in a prison cell in Rome, where he died.

[74]a howling wind a blowin': the pun in French is lost in English. In French the expression is "un vent à décorner les bœufs," which in English translates literally to "a wind [strong enough] to dehorn bulls," which extends the cuckolding topos.

[75]Original footnote: published by Ollendorff.

Georges Lorin, without a college degree, a simple Parisian with a public-school education, loving his Paris, twenty times or more found the entirely special accents for singing his great city unadorned. He is a modernist. Who knows whether, later, poets will know Greek? Sometimes Lorin's feet got tangled up in the poet's toga, and he tore the cloth; then, basta! a pirouette, the *lazzo* of a Parisian street urchin, the sincere tear of a touched spectator of the l'Ambigu[76], and he finds himself a good Parisian of the studio again, sweet dreamer of asphalt, espying in the moonlight the faces that pass by, or also the windows lit up, steering clear of the carriages, and biting his handkerchief to dissimulate sobs. That gentle dreamer was my first buddy... but what a bad president of the Hydropaths! too liberal, too liberal!

Another vice-president, that was Georges Moynet. Another Parisian, born in Versailles, but joyful, and not a versifier for a farthing, – he tried to write an operetta in verse, his collaborator went crazy. Moynet was an architect, and, my faith, he led a joyful life, without care, collecting extraordinary adventures with tranquility. On evenings of professional banquets, he was asked to narrate some of his epic adventures. He gladly accepted and everyone was writhing in laughter.

Brought to the Hydropaths, he was introduced as a first-rate storyteller; he denied it, then, nagged, gave in, and re-improvised those improbable things: *Le Canard, le Phoque, la Bergère Watteau*, and many others. After auditioning – a dream! – the *Hydropath* journal begged him to put those fantastical stories down on ordinary paper, he gave in again, and little by little a collection materialized that the publisher Jules Lévy, the king of incoherents, and a Hydropath himself, published under the title *Entre-Garçons*. Moynet's literary life has done a disservice to architecture, which may have lost in him a Vitruvius;[77] for he had already published the following books which were in the library: *Merveilles, les Merveilles du Théâtre*; but we got an astonishing novel out of him, with a depth of observation

---

[76]Ambigu: Théâtre de l'Ambigu

[77]Vitruvius: Marcus Vitruvius Pollio (81-15 BC), an Roman architect. He wrote a treatise on architecture entitled *De architectura*.

marvelously cruel beneath its gay outward appearance, in a compact, precise, lively style. I take this opportunity to say that *Zonzon* (that's the name of the novel) obtained only one or two write-ups (by Sarcey for example, very good); but Moynet is not so easily taken aback, he will write another novel.

At that time, he put out, to loud outbursts of laughter, a barrage of incredible monologues. He was also vice-president. Ha ha!

There was Grenet-Dancourt, the future author of *Three Woman for One Husband*, that great success, actor and author, who recited Hugo's *l'Aigle du casque*, and by him (with a dark tone to it) *The Grave of the Torture Victim*; then, in his comical tone: *A Terrible Night* or even *Adam and Eve*.[78]

Galipaux, with the monologues written by his friend Paul Bilhaud, unless Paul Bilhaud does not perform them himself.

And then other young pupils from the Conservatory, such as Calmettes, Ruef, Jules Lévy, who has since then become the emperor of the Incoherents,[79] and... a publisher. They recited poems by Sully-Prudhomme, de Silvestre, de Mendès – it was in this way that I learnt by heart *le Consentement*.

Baudelaire, Musset, and Lamartine as well had their great parts to play, and Alfred de Vigny who was butchered sometimes by actors still wet behind the ears, but always applauded by the Hydropath spectators who, freshly graduated from their colleges, completed in this way their poetic education.

The *fumistic* and hullabaloo-ish party was represented by Charles Leroy who, while there, read passages from his *Colonel Ramollot*; by Jules Jouy who, in his voice of a phonograph, detailed his crazy songs and preluded his future successes at the *Chat Noir*.

All that, and many other things besides, were intermingled in a supercharged program.

---

[78]Original footnote: Grenet-Dancourt's monologues have obtained, since then, European and even American renown, as performed by Coquelin aîné. They are published by Ollendorff.

[79]The Incoherents: a short-lived French artistic movement found by Jules Lévy at the end of the nineteenth century.

Sometimes, the president yielded his little bell to Puy-Puy and, re-becoming Émile Goudeau, the author of *Flowers of Bitumen*,[80] recited "The Romans" or "The Greeks" or "The Polish," on the days he was in a good Parisian mood; sometimes, saddened by the unfortunate blows that destiny seldom spares Bohemians, he selected some piece from *Season of Spleen*, "The Long March" for example:

> *I placed it too far, too high, my life's dream,*
> *Beloved future vision and pursued*
> >*Over long days of mourning.*
> *I had left home, joyous, without looking back:*
> *Alas! I put faith in my warrior strength,*
> >*And I had nothing but pride.*
>
> *For a long time, I counted the road's milestones,*
> *And said: By walking in this way, clearly,*
> >*I will arrive there by evening.*
> *And each step followed the other, from valleys to hills;*
> *My dreams were distant, and my stars lofty;*
> >*And the blue sky grew black.*

* * *

> *To desire! To become! that's the law of nature!*
> *To march still and forever! march! If, peradventure,*
> >*You touched your goal with your hand,*
> *Leaving behind you the oasis and the source,*
> *Towards another horizon you would resume your course:*
> >*You must die on a path.*

Sometimes Puy-Puy, the vice-president Count Alfred de P***, carried away by the example, got up, adjusted his monocle and, after having gently adjusted the alignment of his beard à la Henry IV, recited *l'Aiguille*, a story that Barthélemy improvised, one evening, at the Marchioness de Talabot's place, when that lady, a bit quickly, sat down, to her displeasure, on a pin, hidden in a cushion.

---

[80]Original footnote: *Flowers of Bitumen* (1st edition, published by Lemerre). Nth edition, published by Ollendorff.

Here, I give that morsel which, I believe, is rather rare, and in a pleasantly Gallic tone, which we are unused to:

THE NEEDLE

What a strange novelty has happened here!
Lying in wait in the middle of an armchair,
A pin has pierced your naked and white skin,
In a place subtracted from profane glances.

Pardon it, madam, for an involuntary crime,
A crime not committed with a libertine aim,
Doubtless it was thinking to fulfill its ministry,
And not be found guilty for stitching satin.

Thank God! of the fright you conceived
Nothing remains but a poignant memory.
And that incident took a comical turn,
Given it could have ended tragically.

Ah! madam, what a sad adventure for you!
What mourning for your spouse! if, having gone astray,
That needle, trained in the work of tailors,
In lieu of making a stitch, had made a suture.

The Hydropaths changed venues many times. Rue de Jussieu, behind the ferocious animals of the *jardin des Plantes*, hosted them for a long time, then a basement located under the café de l'Avenir, 1, place Saint-Michel; the audience was renewed on several occasions, young poets came: Laurent Tailhade, Jean Moréas, d'Esparbès, Marsolleau, Ajalbert, etc.

As for the public, it would no longer be a question of being Homer enumerate it, the phonebook would suffice at a pinch. Note that every four years, new venues pop up out of that blessed ground called the Latin Quarter, where one becomes an ancestor at the end of five years, and a mummy in ten.

We saw there, from politicians like M. Viette, the minister, to men of science like Dr. Monin, the full gamut of members in the audience. Painters aplenty, Dillon, Willette, Mesplès, René Gilbert, Michel de l'Hay, Luigi Loir, Bastien-Lepage, and others. Then the variety artists like Bryois, alternately theater secretary and traveler to the Congo, etc., etc., etc.

And now let's talk a little about music. Oh! just a few names. The Polish pianist Marylka Krysinska, the marvelous violoncellist Jean Tolbecque, the composer Léo Goudeau (Montancey) who left two or three minor works of which P.P.C. and *Musique éparse* are the best; the organist Maurice Petit, the composer Georges Vuidet, the Swedish violinist Zetterquist, the composer Marcel Legay. A dash here: Maurice Rollinat with his macabre compositions, and his dreadful voice with its two octaves, harsh, strong, perforating. And the subtle Sivry, the gentle cabalist, with an entire orchestra some-times. Then, the master musician, the master singer of the Hy-dropaths, Georges Fragerolle: I cite among his compositions *le Noël* by Jean Richepin, *la Promenade* by Boucher, *le Chat botté*[81] by An-dré Gill, *Si voulez, mademoiselle* by Émile Goudeau; at that period in time, with an incontestable talent, he took the words of the poets and gave them wings with his music, and above all Martin himself sang them with a baritone voice both soft and loud, frank and supple. He was the maëstro of the Hydropaths as he is now of the *Chat Noir*. Other compositions like *la Marche de Macbeth* would suffice to have the measure of him; but he doesn't abuse his talent, and he prefers to sing what sounds clear, and enters the ear smoothly. When will he perform his comic opera?

I can cite nothing by the composers, isn't that right? I hear nonetheless, while writing these lines, a ton of *tradéri, la la la, farafanfan, la la lère...* And then the good fellows sitting at the table. Encore! encore! encore!

But he was a bit of a fumist, that Fragerolle, and set off too many fireworks in the session halls then. Musicians are not perfect.

There were also – O necessary music! – the songs repeated in chorus.[82]

---

[81]*le Chat botté: Puss in Boots*, quoted earlier.

[82]Original footnote: In its September 10, 1887 issue, *The Searchers' Intermediary* asked what were the Hydropathesque songs. Here are some of them then.

For there were two or three clans of Hydropaths: the poet-dreamers, the gay versificators, the hullabalooers and fumists, in addition to the good listeners, the songs adopted are of very different varieties.

To begin with, the two Hydropathesque marches written by Georges Lorin; here are a couple strophes from *The Good Devil*:

> *People with a good head on,*
> > *Party poopers (2x)*
> *Speak quite ill of me,*
> > *I don't care!*
> *In my heart I'm happy,*
> > *At least I think so;*
> *The great queen is the Muse*
> > *Art is the great king...*
> > *I am a good devil!*
> *Ah, ah! come away with me.*

>   * * *

> *In my lair, one resuscitates*
> > *The success (2x);*
> *One does not sing verses*
> > *Cockeyed.*
> *Everyone comes down into the arena,*
> > *Without fear of the tournament.*
> *Sympathy is queen,*
> > *Good sense is king...*
> > *I am a good devil!*
> *Ah, ah! come away with me.*

Then, following the first wave of vacations (because there are vacations in the Latin Quarter), *The Round of Return*:

> *Finally, here are our friends, alternately*
> > *Hydropaths,*
> > *They come as they are,*
> > *On all fours,*
> > *In return.*

Long were your absences!...
De profundis *your absences!*
  One sees, stout,
  Your cohorts,
  Through the doors,
  Returning.

Already, the bow lies in wait for the violins,
  And the artist-
  Pianist
  Follows the trail
  Of round dots!
Farewell then! landscapes,
Lakes, torrents, streams, shores
  Haymakings, ferns,
  Housewives,
  Shepherds,
  The great outdoors...

It is now, to the rhythm of our verse,
  That one evokes,
  Mount, shack,
  Baroque rock,
  Or green prairies.
The president makes a face,[83]
He rings his bell:
  "Silence!
  "Begin!"
  Good luck,
  And break a leg!

That was sung by two hundred voices. Rude effect. Richepin's *Noël* was a great success as well, set to music by Fragerolle.[84]

Noel! Noel! the lovers
Are quite happy; for it is for them

---

[83]Original footnote: Thank you.

[84]Original footnote: *Beggars' Song*, published by Dreyfous.

The gray coat of fog is made;
Ring, bells! bells, ring!
The poor devil, in his nose,
Hears the carillon of colds.

Noel! Noel! the religious
Go on singing, like calves,
Near the donkey round the crib...
Our man would find something newer
To eat than a quarter side of beef,
And says that that smells like fresh meat.

* * *

Noel! Noel! the vicar says
That, among us, God descended
To console the poor wretch...
This one here would quite like
To drink to a good God's health;
But God has put nought in his glass.
            Noel! Noel!

Next to these artistic recitatives, there was the demi-political song, the satire. I ask forgiveness of fallen gods, but that is historical. These words are those of a gentleman, M. de C***, veiled under the pseudonym of de Loya:

We have had, on the throne of France,
Marshals, kings, emperors,
All those men there filched our finances.
T'is no more need, French people, t'is no mistake.
Grévy makes our hearts hope again,[85]
He's wholesome and plays well at billiards;
That's all one needs to govern France
At billiards one does not lose five milliards.

---

[85]Grevy: Jules Grevy (AD 1807-1891) a French politician. Elected President of the Republic in 1879. A Jurassian (a native of Jura, France) he was nicknamed the Jurassic because of his old age.

Refrain:

Our holy Republic is saved
Let's go, French people, with a single cry,
To acclaim Grévy the Jurassic,
Let's cry, French people: Long live Jules Grévy!
             Long live Grévy!

No more Mexico, no more crazy conquests,
No more galas, no more ruinous policies;
All for the people, to him all celebrations
Full of lanterns, flags, discourses;
Our president knows how to deliver good messages,
His diadem is a gibus hat;
And disdaining sumptuous equipages
For six sous, he rides the omnibus.

             Refrain.

One can see with what sort of spirit that was conceived, I will leave off providing the two last couplets, whose topicality alone made it meritorious.

For my own part, I would much prefer the old popular songs, such as *le Cycle du vin*.

The vineyardist goes along planting his vines,
        Plant, let's plant, let's plant wine;
Behold the pretty vine in the wine
        Behold the pretty vine!

From vine to earth! There is the pretty earth!
        Plant, let's plant, let's plant wine;
Behold the pretty earth in the wine!
        Behold the pretty earth!

And from *earth* to *stock*, from *stock* to *branch*, from *branch* to *bunch*, and so on.

        Bunch, let's bunch, let's bunch wine,

Behold the pretty bunch of wine,
Behold the pretty bunch.

From *bunch* to *basket*, from *basket* to *vat*: Behold the pretty *vat*!!! with a suspensive stop. Then from *vat* to *ton*, from *ton* to *pitcher*, from *pitcher* to *pint*, from *pint* to *glass*, from *glass* to *mouth*, and with each word the: Drink, let's drink, let's drink the wine!

Then from *mouth* to *stomach*, and from *stomach* to *piss*.

Piss, let's piss, let's piss the wine!

Finally from piss to earth:

Plant, let's plant, let's plant the wine!

And the cycle can recommence, like every good cycle.

And yet another, in the free and Gallic genre; there are three cannoneers... (pardon, ladies!)

Three cannoneers have exited hell
    One evening through the window! (2x)
It would appear that Lucifer
    Was no longer (2x) their master.
The sentinel who guarded them
    Was a Minim friar. (2x)

He shouted at them three times: halt there!
    Halt there! halt there! Who goes there!
The three cannoneers said to him:
We are three good chaps who piss on your b***.

There was a formidable and soldierlike chorus... And another:

Ah! if the Seine was full of that good Beaune wine,
And if my throat was five-hundred-ell wide,
    I would betake me under a bridge,
    There, I'd stretch myself out;
    And I would make the Seine

Descend into my belly.

And if King Henry wanted to prevent me,
        I would say to him: Good King Henry
            Protect Paris,
        Paris with Vincennes,
        But leave the Seine to me!

The *Marguerite* (or *Madeleine*) doing her hair up with six bottles of wine, already mentioned above, the *Ballad of Jesus Christ Who Dresses like a Poor Man*, and the terrible song of *The Wagoner's Wife*.

Ah! it's the wife, it's the wagoner's wife,
Who goes from door to door, from inn to inn,
        Looking for her husband,
            Shine the light on him
        With a lantern.

She's asking for her husband; her husband is dead drunk and abed with a servant; in tears, she returns to her lodgings, proclaiming her despair:

My poor children, bemoan your ill fortune,
Bemoan your fate to have had such a father;
        I found him in bed,
            Shine the light on her,
        With another mother!

He's done right, the children responded,
He's done right to sleep with the woman he loves;
        And when we are grown up,
            Shine the light on them,
        We'll all do the same!

As an aside, assuredly less ferocious, there was the *Principles of Art* by Charles Cros, which one could hear several couplets of recently at Vaudeville, in *The Clémenceau Affaire*. Here are the sculptors that speak:

Let's proclaim the principles of art,
*   That no one might alter!*
The glazed earth, it's like a lobster.
Once, twice, when it's cooked, it's red.

Let's proclaim the principles of art!
*   That everyone gets drunk!*
The plaster is a bit pale...
Once, twice, but it flows well in the mold...

Let's proclaim the principles of art,
*   That everyone pours out;*
The marble is a matter apart:
Once, twice, there's nothing whiter.

And the principles of art were proclaimed, with the wild cheers of exasperated Gauls, and, sometimes, to add to the tumult, the bard Quellien joined in to let out the cry of the Chouan[86]: Hou-ou-ou-houh!

In a rapid survey, I have tried to give an impression of what those sessions might have been like, when the playfulness of youth was mixed with a strong love of art under its most divers forms.

---

[86]Chouan: a nickname given to a royalist counter-insurgency movement during the French Revolution, based out of Maine, Normandy, and Brittany.

Chapter Nine

Oh! money! – Francisque Sarcey and Jules Claretie. – The Student by F. Champsaur. – Schools. – The Molière by Georges Berry. – A bailiff's burial. – The Naturalist and Modern Review: Harry Alis and Guy Tomel. – Various Debuts. – The Hydropath: Paul Vivien. – Binettes and sonnets. – Tout-Paris. – An evening that does not resemble torture by impalement.

When we had finished dining, at the restaurant, on the boulevard Montmartre, I hailed a ride; a very Parisian comrade said to me then:

"Where can you be going off to so quickly?"

"To preside over the Hydropaths," I responded.

"What do you get for that?"

"Nothing."

"Then," he concluded, "it's stupid!"

It was stupid, it was naïve, that's how it was. I imagined I was fulfilling a mission: instilling into the noggins of young students, destined to become the upper bourgeoisie, notions of poetry and art; to reveal to them books they didn't know about, through the vehicle of public elocution; to force young poets to enter into the lists, like the troubadours of ancient times, like but unlike the troubadours who had knocked on the seigneurial doors of feudal chateaus, only that today it is like addressing oneself, if not to universal suffrage, at least to the restricted suffrage of the next generation of bourgeois leaders, kings of the epoch, to make ourselves known and appreciated.

That bizarre apostolate was complete: lacking any and all literary jealousy, all bias of school, attempting to leave the stage open for all poets, Romantics, Parnassians, Brutalists, Modernists, Symbolists, including Gaulic singer-songwriters, satirists, and even bad poets desirous of launching themselves; everyone had a right to the stage, and the public alone became their judge. No coteries there, nor personal promotion, but a sort of theater of poetry open to all and sundry, and at the same time a field of study for students of the Conservatory (go hang yourself, Bodinier, we had dreamt of the Theater of Application before you had).[87]

A pecuniarily disinterested and – something more difficult still – literarily disinterested program. Would we start up again today, I don't know; but, in any case, what we had done then originated, it must be granted, from a feeling worthy of praise.

I must say that in the face of that criticism directed at my street roots, we had the pleasure, my comrades and myself, of receiving, in the newspaper columns, the praises and encouragements of the press.

Francisque Sarcey wrote this in the *XIXth Century* (December 1878):

> *The young people who have gotten together to found this circle (The Hydropaths) are for the most part budding poets, or students at the School of Fine Arts, or musicians. The club was founded not more than five or six weeks ago, and it counts already nearly two hundred members.*
>
> *It is comfortably installed on rue Cujas... There one recites poetry, plays music, sings and converses... Some young artists have already had the pleasure of attending these sessions, which are fun and gay. Villain (from the Comédie-Française) has done some very amusing impersonations there, that everyone was in raptures over. Coquelin Cadet has performed several of those witty entr'actes that he delivers delightfully and which have had so much success in salons and at concerts. It is likely that once this institution is known, other artists will ask for nothing better than to be heard there, in that very intelligent milieu, all together and very pleasant.*
>
> *Those young people, at a pinch, could get*

---

[87]Bodinier... Theater of Application: Charles Bodinier (AD 1844-1911), director from 1888 of the Théâtre d'Application, a theater for students of the Conservatory, and later from 1890-1902 of La Bodinière, a theater very like the Hydropaths, but for upper class audiences only.

along by themselves. Many are poets, what I mean is they write verse. It is completely natural that one should ask them to read it... That large audience will do more to develop their talent and make them aware of their short-comings, than those little so-called poetic chapels where everyone passes God around when it's their turn, while a half-dozen thurifers fill their noses with incense, provided the same is done for them. Those closed coteries keep their windows carefully shut to the large currents of public opinion. The initiated breathe a subtle and heady air there, where their talent risks withering. The precious refinements of those polishers of verse are not for the public at large, and it is for this reason that I'm quite happy to learn that our young poets of today can read, before a numerous audience, their novel productions.

I hope that many students will aggregate at that club. A young poet remarked to me, not without some bitterness, that, among the students of law or medicine, there are those who, and the most distinguished among them, were still thinking, in terms of poetry, on classical poetry, and who, since graduating college, have read nothing but books in their line of study, or, here and there, the latest novel, and have no idea of the great revolution that V. Hugo set in motion in French poetry, over the course of these last thirty years.

Wouldn't it be to their advantage to participate in that elite group of young artists, some of whom will one day enjoy celebrity, who will become writers or painters or musicians of first order, just as they themselves are destined one day to walk in the footsteps of Allou[88] or Velpeau.[89]

---

[88]Allou: Édouard Allou (1820-1888), a French lawyer and politician.

[89]Velpeau: Alfred Armand Louis Marie Velpeau (AD 1795-1867), a French surgeon and anatomist.

After all, an evening passed there, conversing about art and literature, is at least as agreeable and certainly more useful than wasting one's time playing dominoes at a café table. It seems to me that if I were twenty years old I would look into joining the Hydropaths club.

Among a slew of other articles, quite a few encouragements, even in the form of letters, I cite again – for one has to draw the line somewhere – these lines of correspondence written in *The Belgian Independence* (February 1879), by M. Jules Claretie:

... And the Hydropaths, what is that? It's a kind of club, a literary association on the Left Bank, that seems to grow each day in number and in importance, and which already has its own journal, its own official monitor, l'Hydropath, just as it has its own president, M. Émile Goudeau, a poet, the author of a vigorous volume of verse that is boldly entitled: Flowers of Bitumen. *M. Goudeau is a Perigordian who knew how to render with force his Parisian nostalgias; his poetry has muscle. Wednesdays and Saturdays, he presides then, in a room on the ground floor, rue Cujas, over that gathering of the Hydropaths, where music is performed, poetry recited, or listened to; there are nearly three hundred participants now, compared to thirty from three months ago. Coppée, Monselet, André Gill, Paul Arène, participate sometimes at the Hydropath club, and recite their sonnets or fragments of poems or fantasies, prose and verse. Coquelin Cadet is the spokesperson for a large part of these new comers, he gives them his Britannic phlegm, recites their bouffoneries, or makes their chimeras come alive. He is the applauded champion of the fantastical entr'actes of Charles Cros; the man behind that bizarre, astounding comic with his intense craziness... Moreover he brings with him to the Hydropaths more than one comrade from the Comédie-Française; and, thanks to him, that novel*

gathering, that has no shortage of poetry or passion, recognizes and applauds laughter.

Thus, it may be that, from that ground floor room on rue de Cujas, a literary renaissance for the Latin Quarter will emerge. "There are no more students," says M. Duquesnel, when one asks him about the Odeon[90] and its audiences.

One sees that he's mistaken. Who knows what will become of the Hydropath club, all aboil right now, full of vitality, with its admirations and its violent dislikes? I have no idea, but I see a happy symptom there.

To respond to that need for activity, which a gathering of three hundred young persons caused to ferment, journals and reviews were soon founded, some of which died rapidly, others lasting for years. There was *The Student*, by Félicien Champsaur; *The Schools* by Harry Alis and Guy Tomel, which had a short life; then *The Hydropath* by Paul Vivien, director, and Émile Goudeau, editor in chief; *The Molière* by Georges Berry; *The Plume* by Jean de la Leude; *The Modern Review*, by Harry Alis and Guy Tomel, who had rather long careers, particularly with *The Modern Review*.

This is the place to talk about those journals and reviews.

Félicien Champsaur was one of the youngest, if not the youngest, of the Hydropaths; but restless and audacious like nobody else, with a timid appearance that made him speak with a telegram-like style, or like a little negro. That didn't prevent him from writing some very fine verse, and expressing – in *The Red Moon*, at first with André Gill, then in *The Student*, which he had just founded, – correct and proper ideas, such as those that M. Jules Claretie spoke about in his article in *The Independence,* cited above:

"... Long live the din produced by the beating of twenty-year-old hearts! In a gazette from the Latin Quarter, which goes by the name of The Student, *a new comer, full of passion, prose-writer and poet, M.*

---

[90]Original footnote: See the *Hydropath* journal, same chapter, here below.

Félicien Champsaur, proposes that all theater direc-
tors render a service to youth, at opening nights.
Twenty paid seats that reserved for students. Perhaps
they would spread a little of their fever to those open-
ing nights, always the same, where it's eternally the
pick and the dregs of Paris.

   "And that proposal, which I like, is nothing
new. It was executed at the Odeon in the time of M.
de la Rounat, etc."

At that period of time, F. Champsaur hesitated a little between politics and letters. He frequented Laguerre and Pichon, the
future deputies, as well as André Gill, with whom he was supposed
to create *The Men of Today*; he was one of the first enthusiasts of the
club, and the *Hydropaths*, where he came to recite sonnets of an often exquisite modernism, and which appeared in *l'Événement* and
elsewhere before being collected in a volume published by Lemerre.

   The Schools, founded by Harry Alis and Guy Tomel, did not
last long; but the two young associates learned the profession of
managing director, an experience that allowed them later to make
The Modern Review last four years, which I will speak about a little
later.

   The Plume, by Jean de la Leude, had the Hydropath Edmond
Deschaumes for secretary, whose columns have since then been so
remarked on at *Réveil, l'Écho de Paris, l'Événement, Mot d'Ordre,*
and, in the meantime, at the *Chat Noir* journal. *The Plume* – bizarre
title – didn't last; one soon called that review *la Revue artistique et
littéraire*, and because it possessed an emerald cover, *la Revue Verte*.

   Le Molière, by Georges Berry, presently a municipal councillor, had a short-lived existence; nevertheless, that journal had for
collaborator Clairville, the celebrated Clairville (he was still famous
at that time). The death of that Vaudeville player was the occasion of
a bizarre adventure. Georges Berry and the director of *le Molière*
were supposed to attend the funeral of that master of *flonflons*. They
departed late and arrived at the church. There, they were hidden in
the crowd. The director of *le Molière,* very ignorant about Paris, recognized or thought he recognized in the assembly Victor Hugo, Re-

nan, Émile Augier, Mme. Anaïs Ségalas, Emmanuel Gonzalès, and *tutti quanti*; prudent and already political, Georges Berry recognized no one. The ceremony was concluded, the two directors of *le Molière* jumped into a funeral carriage, and reached Père-Lachaise cemetery. There, grave and contemplative – Berry looking in vain for anyone he might know among the assembly, while his young co-director caught sight of Madeleine Brohan or Coquelin Cadet, farther off Barbey d'Aurevilly or Burani, – there, grave and contemplative, they found a place in the front row, on Clairville's tomb, to listen to the discourse, the funeral oration. A man with graying hair approached them on the embankment.

"That's Émile Augier," whispered the co-director.

"Shh!" said Georges Berry, who continued not to recognize anyone.

The man with graying hair began:

"The man, whom we are all lamenting, was a model of his profession, alas! too denigrated. He had at one and the same time the dignity and the style of that profession, so necessary to the security of transactions..."

"Where are we?" thought Berry.

"... transactions, which ought to be the rule, but which so often are a prey to the faithless parties to a contract. We suffer the discredit!... But, gentlemen, those who discredit us are precisely those who ought to have no credit... Ah! Gentlemen! before this tomb so prematurely open, I would like to be able to express just what this honest, upright, unrelenting life is for men who represent the Gates of Justice; for stamped paper is none other than the sword of modern Law, and, as our titles indicate, we are guards of the sacred Door to the temple of Law. To speak ill of the bailiffs of justice..."

"Oh!" said Georges Berry, "let's get out of here."

"But why," responded the co-director; Émile Augier speaks very well.

"Let's go! let's go!" said Berry.

They cleared off. They had mistaken the chapel, and had followed the funeral of a bailiff.

I was at the time an editor of *le Molière;* but I didn't go to Clairville's funeral.

I was also – oh! for a short instant – secretary of *The Naturalist and Modern Review*. It was called *modern* from the beginning, then *Naturalist*, in order to please Harry Alis, who was attached to the obligatory school of Zola – obligatory at that time! O how time flies!

That was for the *Hydropaths*, simple speakers of verse, a debut occasion in typographical form, beside those who had already been printed and applauded. I find among the acclaimed and known names, who had arrived or at least were no longer virgins to publicity: Paul Bourget and Maupassant. Bourget's verse and also a study on Renan.[91]

From his hermitage on rue Guy-de-la-Brosse, the gentle poet, the delicate analyst who was destined to become the profound psychologist of the novel, left his home sometimes to visit the Hydropaths, and he treated us to several poems. I cite one randomly:

SONNET

If ever there was a means to dishonor the soul,
It is to love an unworthy woman, and to hear,
At the tender and ecstatic moment of pleasure,
In her voice, an echo of her infamous profession.

Those words interspersed with ardent sighs,
She exhales them coldly, leisurely,
To excite the senses and lash the desires,
Into the ears of those who pay to hear her swoon.

And then, they have gripped that beautiful body, all naked,
They have kissed her mouth, kissed her skin,
Their hands have caressed her flesh abandoned to them...

---

[91]Study on Renan: See Bourget's *Essais de Psychologie Contemporaine*, published by Lemerre, 1885.

Ah! why is there no lustral water, no strong wine,
O woman, to heal the impassioned soul,
Or to rejuvenate you and wash away your blood.

Guy de Maupassant, who, all the while frequenting the evening gatherings at Médan, had not yet produced that masterpiece *Boule-de-Suif*, was still looking to find his voice in poetry; one of his pieces, entitled *The Girl*, had nearly caused the *la Revue* to pass under the knout of justice.

In the same issue, J.-K. Huysmans had inserted a short study entitled *Parisian Symphonies*. But they debuted, if I'm not mistaken, Paul Alexis – the future Trublot[92] of *le Cri du Peuple*[93] – with his *les Femmes de M. Lefèvre*; Edmond Deschaumes, with a short story *A French Nihilist*; Buillaumel, that is to say Guillaume Livet (*Mirliton* from *Gil-Blas* and *l'Événement*), *la Fabrication d'un roman*; Paul Lordon (*le Diablotin* in *l'Écho de Paris)* with dramatic critiques; Dubut de Laforet with a short story, *Dans les champs*; Maurice Guillemot, Detouche and Fragerolle (chance critic, musician by profession), and my poor dear brother Léo Goudeau, he also a musician, become a writer under the pseudonym of Léo Montancey (he worked himself to death); and Vaste Ricouard, and the masters of prose, Harry Alis, Guy Tomel, and Champsaur. For poetry, I see the poets who have disappeared, like Jules Aubry – a serious professor of law, living elsewhere in France today – with *les Moulins de pierre*, of which I wish to cite the first stanzas:

You are the magnificent giants of the plain,
O old windmills resting on your elbows on the ground,
And, in the fields bathed in a serene light,
I love to see your bare profiles standing there.

I love your conical rooves and your grey walls,

---

[92]Trublot: the pseudonym, or *nom de plume*, that Alexis used when publishing his work in *le Cri du Peuple*. It was also the name of a character (Hector Trublot) in Zola's *Pot-Bouille*.

[93]*le Cri du Peuple*: a journal famously founded, and widely read, during the Paris Commune, until suppressed; later it was resumed from 1883-1888. It is in this second appearance of the journal that Alexis was published.

And the fight of birds that graze your flanks,
And your canvas wings when the breeze blows,
And your millers like white ghosts.

My eye often enjoys, o my good turrets,
To see in the sonorous air, filled with shivers,
Your gigantic wings slowly turning,
When the rising wind bends the crops.

You are the joyful laborers that the breeze
Animates incessantly with large fan strokes,
And you gladden my soul, O churchless steeples,
Everyday when the mass for labor sounds...

　　　* * *

I would have also liked to cite the first verses by Théodore Massiac[94] who, today, writes forewords to dramatic works for the *Gil-Blas*; and the debuts of Trézenick, author of the *Gouailleuses*; of Lemouël (poet of *Feuilles au vent*, and illustrator for the *Chat Noir*); of Gustave Vautrey (who, in collaboration with Livet, had an act put on at the Odeon), and of Clovis Hugues, the fierce tribune, – they all placed their verse in good order under the Hydropathic banner that *The Naturalist and Modern Review* held high and firm. And what's this? I see the ears of a decadent pricking up – oh! no, not decadent nor deliquescent, he'd be too upset with me – of a symbolist, Gustave Kahn.

It's a poem in prose that begins like this:

"Absinthe, mother of happiness, O infinite liquor, you shimmer in my glass like the pale green eyes of the mistress I once loved. Absinthe, mother of joy, like Her, you leave in the body a memory of distant sorrows; absinthe, mother of mad rages and staggering drunkenness, when a man can, without thinking himself crazy, call himself loved by his mistress. Ab-

---

[94]Original footnote: Massiac devised, after a very old custom, putting lowercase characters at the head of his lines of verse.

sinthe, your perfume cradles me..."

That ends like this:

*"The sleazy dive is big, square, and on the barrels
with their round bellies the gaslight flickers its light,
and at the wooden tables, poor, ill-clad men, made
ugly in the light, chat and smoke pipes...*

*"...And schoolboys come there, to smoke illegally the
pipe that they will stash there, there, next to a wall.
They leave, the schoolboys, their stomach all upset,
but proud to have hung from their teeth the clay pipe
that they'll leave there, next to a wall.*

*"The sleazy dive is square, long, full of light and
smoke."*

Maurice Rollinat also gave very often, to *The Review,* pieces
performed at the Hydropaths club; and, as for myself, poems or
prose, I submitted, either under my name or under the pseudonym of
Diègo Malevue, or Dr. Servet, what equated to a large in-octavo volume.

The Naturalist and Modern Review, located at the outset on
the fifth floor of rue Blanche, came to be lodged on the ground floor
of rue Monsieur-le-Prince, before it changed location again to rue
Grange-Batelière where, after two years and several months, it ex-
pired, having been administered Hydropathic sacraments and wept
for by all those who knew it.

That was certainly the most serious effort by the Society to
come together in digest form; but what made the strength of the Hydropaths, inasmuch as a very numerous gathering, was the absence
of imposed doctrines, the personalism of its adherents, their independence. For in a *Review*, on the contrary, it seems necessary to speak
of an absolute doctrine that one imposes on it or that one makes the
readers accept. For the reader is led in a particular direction by its esthetic, whereas the spectator accepts everything. There is, between
the subscriber and the casual spectator, as much difference as between an amateur appreciator of paintings that make up a gallery and

he who visits the Salon and museums, letting himself go with his changing and animated impressions.

Besides, too much juvenile audacity in a *Review* grates on the ear, since the term "Review" has become synonymous with extreme Jansenism. A *Review* should have ample skirts, and ought to go forth without showing its thighs.

The *Hydropath* journal was not serious, perhaps not enough, and sometimes lapsed into pure *noise*. What was the editor in chief thinking? Alas! He had but a mediocre authority over the terrible creole Paul Vivien, who was its director, sponsor, impresario, facto- tum, its life in a word; nor the discerning Georges Lorin who, under the pseudonym of Cabriol, was the appointed illustrator of Hydro- pathic personalities, and chose his heroes as he pleased; finally – hard thing to admit – that editor in chief had not exercised perhaps enough authority over *himself*, letting himself go as the mood took him with his burlesque fantasies, forgetting sometimes, all too often, the sacred interests of Art that were confided in me. Not a pontiff for a *sous*, that ferocious president... A gendarme over sessions, in order to ensure that people were respected, and imposing silence on the undisciplined; but, outside of the curule chair, standing agape on his own account, and, tendering even – alas! alas! alas! – his resignation as a functionary in the face of the minister of finance, who remained impassive (isn't that right, Léon Say?), so much did that bureaucrat- poet believe in the future.

The *Hydropath journal* published, then, on each... on each what, actually?... each time it appeared, the caricature of a hy- dropath, chosen from among five hundred by the eclecticism of Cabriol, poet and illustrator. There was that of the president natural- ly; then André Gill, Félicien Champsaur, Coquelin cadet, Charles Cros,... Sarah Bernhardt (yes, Sarah! Sarah was a Hydropath), Charles Lomon, Maurice Rollinat, Vacquerie, Luigi Loir, Mélandri, Frémine, Charles Leroy, Grenet-Daucourt, Moynet, Guy Tomel, Vil- lain, Gustave Rivet, Alphonse Allais, Galipaux, Sapeck, Bastien- Lepage, Fernand Icres, Emile Cohl, etc.

One could have left many other medallions for posterity: Paul Arène, Coppée, Bourget, Clovis Hugues, Paul Marrot, Paul Mounet, Harry Alis, Lebargy, and many others; but the journal, despite its intermittence, lived no more than one year and a half; it was a lapse of time really insufficient to construct a Pantheon.

In order to repair, as much as can be done with a quill, that omission in print, I draw telegraphic silhouettes: Paul Arène is of medium height, thin as a rail, and active like a devil, with a pointed beard, soft eyes, and mocking mouth; Coppée, Bonaparte (that's the cliché), dreamer in solitude, gay in Paris; no beard; Paul Bourget, tall, very gentle, blond mustache; Clovis Hugues, short, a shock of hair, bearded, his face having undergone some volcanic trembling; Paul Marrot, short, black beard and hair, a Saracen, obliged to flee Charles Martel, and forgotten at Poitiers by some Maghrebian; Paul Mounet, another Saracen, but big, strong like a Turk (naturally); Harry Alis, English type, tall, cold, with a smooth chestnut-colored beard; Lebargy (go see him at *La Comédie-Française*)... I could go on and on at length, in the same manner; you would hardly gain much thereby.

In the issues of the *Hydropath* journal, following the carica-ture, where everyone is painted brick-red, in the style of Etruscan pictures, I put together several sonnet-silhouettes, some by Jouy, many by Cabriol, others by this one or that one.

Here's what was allotted to the president in the first issue. One will not say that the Hydropaths were a society of mutual praise. With what disrespect Grenet-Daucourt treats his superior:

> *His beard is black, black, and his forehead high, austere,*
> *His nose is ordinary, his eyes haggard;*
> *He has an alert mind and is fleet as a firecracker,*
> *The Hydropaths fear him, and keep quiet and venerate.*
>
> *He's talkative like a monastery porter,*
> *But he does not like others' noise; and knows the art*
> *Of quieting the tempest with a bolivar,*
> *That he wears on his pate, grim and severe.*
>
> *He's a bit of a bear and a knotty stick:*
> *"Oh! he's an imbecile and me! that makes two!"*
> *He says, and the Hydropaths shudder before him.*

He writes poems that are fine, so fine that nobody
Understands them. He is hard, noble, timbred, beautiful.
His name rolls off our tongues... huh? yes... it's Émile.

In that same first issue, there is this sonnet-program by Jules
Joey.

Leave the discreet restaurant where you dined,
Niniche and you, empty and pretentious bourgeois;
Profiting by the lorgnette which wine under your eyes
Poses, come with me and sit down at the Hydropaths.

However, before entering, one word: – that you be amazed
Or no, keep your sententious phrases to yourself,
Before that stream of curious profiles;
The place is informal, one does not take airs.

Indeed, don't expect to find a drop of water
In the shouting parliament that Goudeau presides over;
Let the smell of pipes fill your hirsute nose;

And – less sottish than Louis, with canons all the same,
Striking down the Téniers and their funny types –
Of the Hydropathesque Club, admire the Barbary apes.

In the fourth issue, one sees the smiling face of Coquelin
cadet; a sonnet by Cabriol (G. Lorin).

Coquelinin, coquelinant,
Good Coquelin with the joyful laugh,
The Hydropath – that you must read –
Pays you a fine compliment.

Good little cadet, cackling
The stories that only Cros can write,
That only Coquelin can deliver;
Good cadet, loved to distraction.

Greetings, brand new member!
But do not be silent for us,

To live we need your squeaky fiddle.

Pirouette[95] of the word,
Don't take your role so seriously...
The French... would die of grief.

In issue number 14, that of Charles Frémine, a fine sonnet by Rollinat.

You, you look into the azure, and me into the abysses,
And, while my poems full of fog and bile
Smell of death, debauchery, and crime,
Yours smell of honey and fresh milk.

Me, I set horror to infernal rhymes,
And I bury a morbid scalpel into my heart;
You, you sing love, and you express beauty;
Satan never paid you a nocturnal visit.

And yet my mind inclines over your soul,
And my tenebrous spleen, when I open up to you,
In the arms of your gaiety, for an instant falls asleep.

It's that you, radiant, and me, riddled with alarms,
We both warm up to Art, that golden sun
That sheds its light on hideousness as well as charms.

And in issue number 16, that sonnet by Cabriol to Grenet-Dancourt (too bad, Grenet, I give you what you gave to me).

I do not know if his mistress,
Each evening makes a scene
For his profile. But, if he addresses
Himself to the directors... goodbye scene.[96]

---

[95] Original footnote: Pirouette is, as one knows, Cadet's literary pseudonym.

[96] Original footnote: Since then, that regrettable prognostic had been given the lie to, eleven thousand times by *Three Women for One Husband.*

Too ugly to find a Maecenas[97]
To guide his art that is fussed on,
He can throw himself into the Seine.
To please, he'll need to be reborn.

Up close, however, the pupil
Is velvety and almost pretty;
And then, finally, to seduce us,

– In a pun that comprises
The man – for wit, one can say
He is a Grenet of abundance.

In that issue number 16, with lots of fracas and joy it was announced that the first prize for comedy was awarded to the Hydropath Lebargy. And Cabriol, under the various pseudonyms of Balthazar or Rirenbois, Georges Lorin finally, asked for the decoration of the Legion of Honor for... Sarah Bernhardt.

In issue number 20, the illustration on the cover is of Émile Taboureux (who signed his columns *Mahori* at the *Figaro* some times) is accompanied by an amusing sonnet by Cabriol.

It's the sapper from the regiment
Of the lyre... subsequently!
And his smile at any moment
Proves that he's not tormented.

That smile, it is his mustache
With handlebars attached
To it. He's got a plume for an axe
And, from time to time, a panache.

His gaiety, from prose to verse,
Flirts... with his cap on sideways,
A nice guy for all the world.

It's why he's sung in rounds,

---

[97]Maecenas: Gaius Maecenas, a patron of the arts and friend of Caesar Augustus.

While toasting: "Let them be happy,
Those there who are Taboureux!"

Taboureux remained the veritable loyalist of the Latin Quarter. It's an eternal vocation of youth.

In that same issue, and by contrast, to show that one often mixed tears with laughter, in that *shrill parliament* of the Hydropaths, is found the verse that Charles Cros entitles:

TO LOVERS

Make love, be beautiful, because you can
        In spite of hatreds,
Forget, between two kisses, the reproaches,
        And impending deaths.
Run through the woods, eat blackberries, and cull
        Discreet flowers
In the field; decorate with their petals
        Your beautiful heads.
Or even, go to theaters, under the gaslights,
        In fine places.
Without listening to the drama: "Alas! my mother, alas!"
        Bring opera glasses.
Be surprised, ignorant, against the world,
        What does it matter?
For the wind, as long as you write these verses,
        Will carry them.
You, my dear fellow, love her, look at her, multiply
        Her portrait on
A thousand canvases, painted with the colors of snake skins
        And stars.
And you, whom I see again, when closing my eyes,
        Be happy,
Without worrying about the pluviose grave
        I dig for myself.

In the discreet irony of these lines, the grave and gentle poet sings love lost, sends his counsel to his happy rival, and a discreet tear to Her who has forgotten him, as later, several years later, in

wide stanzas of a contained emotion, he will speak of the death of
his dearly beloved and departed.

It is a dolorous impressionism, and Charles Cros really
should serve as a master to the neophytes of symbolism.

In issue number 18, there's Georges Moynet who resembles,
physically, trait for trait, Émile Zola, as a young man. The impas-
siveness, and the good naturedness of that plumpish narrator earned
him a crazy success, that the sonnet by Grenet-Dancourt certifies:

He chuckles that one confuses him
With a cask of cognac;
Or a tin of tobacco even,
His ruddy person.

His loquaciousness is without parallel;
With the joyful pleasure of a mahou,
He gaily empties his sack
Of mischievousness on the world.

Quite often death
And the cruelties of fate sing;
Him, he makes corsages burst,

And faces dilate.
– "Everyone," he says, "recognizes
That laughter was BORN WITH ME."

In issue number 22, it's Guy Tomel, the professor I so
bizarrely met at fickle Nini-Tamar's place; he's the founder of *la Revue moderne*, a staunch Hydropath, whom an illness of the lungs
forced to leave Paris for Algeria, where he sells dates, oranges, and
wine (oh! wholesale), thus saluted by Cabriol:

BON VOYAGE TO GUY TOMEL

You go away and you leave us,
Bronchitis between your arms;
But you'll come back to us strong!
Our fears will be far then.

That you might better acquit yourself,
Go!... to the land of Saharas.
You'll bring back for me when you come
A rhyme rich in quittances.

Hydropathesque Saint John,
Speaks of us to the Lion
Gens, but belatedly;

And drawing on your fine discourses,
In the country of Algeria,
Make our old bears *be accepted.*

He did it, in fact, with zeal, mention our names to the colonists, at conferences. He did even better and offered an asylum to Léo Goudeau-Montancey, when, worn down by illness, the poor musician went to request a little sunlight and warmth from Algeria, before dying. The Auvergnat Guy Tomel, in an ironical mood, is the warmest person we have ever met, and I must seize the opportunity to tell it to him.

I hardly want to give the impression of someone droning on and on while reading off a list of winners, so I'll hurry it up: here's Eugène Lemouël, the author of *Feuilles au vent*, then Villain, the *great* Villain embellished by a rondeau by André Gill:

RONDEAU

That was villainous? No, but it was irregular,
And, from behind the fog, it came straight
At me. I told myself while rubbing my eyes:
"Eh! But it's the obelisk, indubitably,
That has just stayed out all night – farcical monument! –
And by dawn returns to the plinth it inhabits."
Now, as I stepped aside very quickly,
The object out of the mist emerged brusquely...
*   It was Villain!*

He had stayed out all night, by golly! the sybarite;

I had then, to a degree, prejudged wisely,
And I claim here all the honor that
A precise observation merits; only,
That was not a steeple, nor a peak, nor a monolith...
It was Villain!

In that issue 24, the premature death of the young poet Victor Zay was announced, he who gave more than just hope. Alas! he was the first among us to disappear...

Let's move on, move on quickly: or that list of winners risks turning into a necrological compendium. Farewell, poor little Victor Zay, you who were so proud to wear a ribbon of black velvet, fifteen centimeters wide, on your hat. It was a crepe of black mourning that he should have had. Let's move on, move on!

There was Gustave Rivet, the poet, the author of a drama, *le Châtiment*, staged with success at Cluny, the deputy Rivet, the under-secretary of State, etc., etc.

Then Alphonse Allais, whom the *fumists* recognized as their veritable leader, since Sapeck's voluntary exile, and who is now editor in chief of the *Chat Noir Journal*.

Galipaux, not much higher than that and who has become a star at *la Renaissance*, while writing such amusing volumes, such as *Galipètes* and *la Tournée*.

And now Sapeck, with the biography by Alphonse Allais: Sapeck had just been the hero of a bizarre adventure. He had gotten it into his head to dye his hair red, not a modest red, but a bright, fiery red, blood red; he had a yellow vest made for himself, short culottes, and, donning a Scottish fur hat, he promenaded in the Jardin du Luxembourg. His apparition excited such a stir, so enormous a frenzy in the crowd, that the guards seized him, despite his resistance, and handed him over to the gendarmes who were watching the palace, who confided him to the neighborhood policemen, who finally led him to the station.

We went there several hours later to bail him out; now, he was unable to exit, because he had belonged: 1st to the minister of the interior, in the hands of the guards of the Jardin du Luxembourg, from which the connection to the minister; 2nd to city of Paris, from the moment that the gendarmes had laid hands on him; 3rd to the prefecture of Police, and 4th, by association, to the ministry of justice of Paris. There was a competition among those diverse powers. It took twelve hours for them to come to an agreement and sort it out. Strange, no? But quite administrative.

And here is the illustrator Émile Cohl, the testamentary executor of poor André Gill, to whom he had dedicated a volume (published by Vanier).

Maurice Petit, sub-organist of the church des Invalides; and who was at one time president of the *Hirsutes*, that society born from the ashes of the Hydropaths.

Bastien-Lepage, the glorious painter, dead in his prime.

Finally, Fernand Icres, the author of *Mitron*, from *Les Fauves*, who at first had his poetry read by Lebargy; then risked reading it himself, despite the worst Pyrenean accent human ears have ever heard, especially when he declaimed the piece entitled *l'Ancienne*, beginning like this:

Two years of soppy and affected love,
Were unable to chase the montagnarde
From the memories of my past.
And I awoke, unable
To forget her flanks and thighs
Stretched out beside the grave.

Imagine a Marseillais, mixed with a Spaniard, and sprinkled with Auvergnatism, reciting that verse: *Deux angu... n'ont poingu... oublier son flangue... S'étalangnt*. It was terrible. Then that bizarre rule, imposed by one does not know whom, requiring pure Meridionals to pronounce *fiaule* for *fiole* and *drale* for *drôle*, a *saule frite* and a *sole pleureur!!* Does it not seem to you that there exists down there, among us, a special institution dedicated to the deformation of sounds? One would seem to think. Eh, well! that bizarre accent, given the nature of Icres' poems, contributed positively to his success, much to the astonishment of the delicate Lebargy.

From this last issue, I present that fanciful quatrain written in the guest register of the Fatouville lighthouse (near Honfleur) by Georges Lorin (Cabriol):

Just as there are genteel woman,
There are also bitter puns!
Makeup illuminates the filles,
The lighthouse illuminates the seas.

The *Hydropath* journal, which bore the subtitle *Tout-Paris* on its last three issues, passed away – it also! – in the month of June 1880, in a printshop in Sceaux, while the air, perfumed with the scent of lilacs, invited us to live on. Alas!

But that was not at all the fault of its founder, Paul Vivien. No. He dispensed his time and his money to sustain that illustrated journal. Unfortunately, the ambition to do something great sunk us. A young man who boldly assumed the pseudonym of Joinville (ex-cellent name of a director of columns, provided he always got his *Five Louis*), having come into some money, declared that he wanted to enlarge, restore, transform, ennoble *The Hydropath Journal*, by moving it to a locale on the Right Bank, 40, rue Richelieu, in the fourth arrondissement, with a new name, *Tout-Paris*, etc., etc. Hopes, dreams, illusions!

Joinville played at baccarat even more than as Maecenas. That was our downfall.

The opening of the new locale was moreover accompanied by inauspicious events. I will tell the story just as it happened:

Joinville and his faithful Achates[98], Gabriel R...., had launched a series of invitations in the world of arts and letters: *Tout-Paris*[99] had to be there. It was a question even of pursuing certain artists in carriage. I was responsible for Tolbecque and his violoncel-lo. Towards nine o'clock, the musician and I, we descended before the carriage entrance. The concierge took care of the instrument; we began to climb, rapidly, the staircase of *Tout-Paris*. To the fourth

[98]Achates: the faithful companion of Aeneas.

[99]*Tout-Paris*: in the sense of all of Paris, everyone who was anyone in Paris.

floor! Horrible! Key in the lock, nobody inside, not a light... not a soul!... and darkness!... What to say? I went back downstairs, trembling, asked the concierge for a candle. I made some light, a dim light, going among the pieces of furniture, along the wall-hangings, my feeble light casting enormous shadows, armed by dark phantoms, the only inhabitants of that lodging. Tolbecque sat down, impassive.

The sound of steps on the stairway. Here's the actor Montbars, Coquelin cadet, Daubray... Their astonishment joins ours, like a coefficient, and transforms it into stupefaction. More steps on the stairway. Now journalists, poets, singers. We are now twenty people now huddled around a single candle planted in a candelabra with five arms. The jokes were heavy: but we laughed. Someone uncovers a basket of champagne in another room. Another person finds glasses. On a table, we set down the candelabra, and we drink. And still more steps on the stairway... Forty people now. Vivien, sad at first, writhes in laughter finally.

A fleet step... Ah! I grabbed Gabriel R... in the antechamber. "What's going on?"

"... Spent the whole day at the gambling table! Forgot the hour! Lost! won! lost again! lost everything!"

"Everything? Oh!"

"Joinville won't have access to funds until tomorrow."

"Where is he?"

"He's out looking... looking... looking... for money... for victuals... for drinks... for light..."

"Where?"

"At his mistress'... a steeple chaser... the Circus... d'Été... Mazeppa!..."

A step, two steps, on the stairway, heavy steps. Is it Blucher, or Grouchey?... It was Grouchey. Saved!

Mazeppa, Joinville, domestics, osier baskets, lobsters, bottles of wine, and... yes, candles!... a circus groom lights them. Light! Finally!

The evening was charming. Verse and songs, piano and vio-loncello, laughter and an improvised supper.

About one in the morning, on exiting that festival-concert that, at the opposite side of the pale, had begun so poorly but fin-ished so well, a group determined to keep on talking about Sarah Bernhardt broke the window of the café of the Théâtre-Français.

The police station was not faraway. Happily, the *Tout-Paris* editorship possessed a creole, a kind of negro, well-dressed, who was required to stay in the slammer for the others. One went to ask about him on the following day, and... Joinville having been ap-proached, the bail was paid... Mazeppa also was reimbursed, fortu-nately: my God!

That didn't prevent the journal from succumbing later to slaughter, the firing squad, and burning at the stake.

Chapter Ten

The journal The Globe. – The Revenge of the Beasts. – The Figaro. –
*The Society for the protection of animals.-- Conferences. – The pha-
lanstery. – Camille's imprecations. – The duel with* liquidium iodide. –
Celebration at Bois-Colombes. – The encounter with Rodolphe Salis.

Ah, well! believe it or not, neither the Hydropathic sessions, nor the
journals, nor the reviews, in spite of the enormous satisfactions of
self-esteem that they gave to my naïvely ecstatic brain of a Parisiani-
fied Meridional, didn't feed my stomach, alas! habituated to four
meals a day since middle school.

Having made the mistake of tossing my resignation into the
face of the ministry of finance (in actuality, to be frank, I hadn't resigned, but had made myself available to other opportunities), I had
to struggle against the elements and necessity: rain or famine, cold or
thirst, like a savage.

For a time, my brother, Léo Goudeau, recently graduated
from Saint-Cyr and who was garrisoned at the barracks of Château-
d'Eau, was able to aid me in that enterprise. But, having suddenly
fallen in love with a Polish woman, a great musician, he who had already been keen on music, felt he had to turn in *his* resignation. –
Could that be a family illness? – That was into the face of the minister of war that his resignation happened to be flung. I was saddened
by it; for, if the reviews and the Hydropathic journals didn't feed
their man, their president even, music didn't seem to me as though it
would be a milk cow... And in fact it wasn't.

Very fortunately, through Paul Bourget's intervention, I entered the *Globe*, where I was assigned the task of going through the
provincial journals.

It was then that I was able to work again. I became the happy
president again. Everything seemed to be coming together. *The Figaro* serialized *The Revenge of the Beasts.* I held a series of conferences at the Salle des Capucines, and *The Revenge* was – o marvel! –
awarded by the Society for the Protection of Animals: a silver medal.

The Hydropaths had held a session at Pierre Petit Hall; what can I say? following a conference given on them at the Capucines, the terrible Hydropaths walked up and down the boulevard, shouting extravagant songs before the flabbergasted bystanders and didn't stop until reaching a café in the faubourg Montmartre, where a café owner, who had recently set up shop, offered them an enormous punch. What else happened? Solicited by the Society for the Protection of Animals, I became, in the middle of the day, an improv actor, and recited that *Revenge* before four thousand *protectors*, installed on the tiered seating of the Cirque d'Hiver. The mania for greatness took me again, but I didn't turn in my resignation to the *Globe*; I sent my brother in my place. He knew quite well how to fill a hole: having been first a military man, then a musician, he improvised as a journalist, much more quickly than a poet could have. Under the pseudonym of Léo Montancey, he entered employment at the *Figaro*, and from there the quotidian *Triboulet*.

Now, while these prosaic successes saved a part of the family, the poetic successes, out of pure vanity, had thrown me back onto the sonorous pavement, and again I heard the vague songs of bitumen.

It was at that time that I met the Blanquist[100] B***l. That Blanquist had always had the idea of founding a phalanstery. He opened up to me, I highly approved of that project: we only talked about it. Two poor men are stronger when united, and twelve poor men are enormous and influential. Such was our reasoning. We were already two indigents, we didn't have to go far to discover eight others, of which one woman, Marylka the Polish woman. In a phalanstery, a woman is indispensable: the cooking and mending. The good Blanquist B***l was the tenant of a sixth-floor flat, rue Catherine-d'Enfer (it must be named something else today, little does it matter). Apart from the young student Br*** who was nicknamed *Pacha*, because his father was an engineer in Constantinople; apart from that *pacha*, who absolutely wanted to be adjoint-cook in order to assist Marylka in the shucking of legumes, the other domestic responsibilities were assigned by lot. Fate designated me as dishwasher. I didn't feel, I confess, drawn to that vocation; but I had to obey.

---

[100]Blanquist: someone who subscribes to the socialist, revolutionary philosophy of Louis Auguste Blanqui.

On the first day I applied a certain zeal in the execution of it; then I relaxed, and some noticed with bitterness that the plates, dishes, forks, – apart from those that were reserved for me – didn't absolutely shine. My cold egoism was severely criticized, and I was deprived of legumes. I didn't give a fig for legumes at that time. Then they deprived me of everything else but bread. I resigned myself to that with more difficulty. Then I thought up a stratagem. Feigning weakness, quite natural for a poorly nourished phalansterian, and a clumsiness due to anemia, I broke three or four plates while washing them, and cracked several glasses. That was it; they chased me from my position, and assigned me... to coal. That consisted in my going to seek various combustibles at the Auvergnat's. I hadn't but a single high hat for those expeditions, and that must have been an unusual spectacle, when I passed, my pail in hand, and faggots under the arm.

Pacha and the *Polish woman* no longer saw eye to eye, what's more, in the preparation of the meal. It was agreed that they would each have their day. Now, when it was the Polish woman's day of service, *Pacha* affected not to eat, finding everything execrable; the Polish woman, in turn, fasted when *Pacha* cooked. It was frightening!

That phalanstery ended up by dissolving under the burden of debts. The association is nothing more perhaps than an empty word. If I have brought up that attempt at Saint-Simonianism here, it's because an absolutely fantastic story is attached to it.

There was a young man, small and slender, who came to see us from time to time. When he wanted breakfast, he brought eggs. We called him Camille because – unexpected thing! – he was in the habit, over desert, over coffee, it didn't matter when, of declaiming the *Imprecations of Camille*,[101] when the subject turned to literature. Strange! strange! but that's how it was!

He was persuaded to come to the Hydropaths club to recite that splendid monologue by Corneille. Camille needed no coaxing. Ah! that was a beautiful evening! Alerted by I don't know whom, the fumists had put their heads together, and Camille was an instant success, he was covered in flowers, he was buried with crowns. B***l, the good Blanquist, had been unable to attend that triumph,

---

[101]Imprecations of Camille: from *Horace* (1640), a play written by Pierre Corneille.

and, the following day, as a joke, he began to rail against me, pretending that I should have let him know; a pretend quarrel ensued, in Camille's presence, who tried in vain to break it up.

In brief! a duel was settled on, after the word *bourgeois* was dropped, thrown by one of us into the other's face.

Preparations for the duel – all the Hydropaths being in on the secret of the mystification, I entreated Camille to be my witness and other roles were assigned to different members of the phalanstery. The Polish woman made the *charpie* and, as she was rather often taken by mad laughter, she pretended that it was nervous. A pistol from the middle ages was the weapon of choice, from thirty paces. The witnesses decided that the encounter would take place in the vague terrain of the Jardin du Luxembourg, which allowed us to sign and date, without lying, our statements as from the frontier of Luxembourg. Camille objected that the policemen would arrest us; while he was insisting, fearing that the noise would attract representatives of authority, we shut him up by a learned dissertation on the topic of *liquidium iodide*, which makes pistols go off without making any noise.

In brief! While the witnesses were arguing over the conditions, and the Polish woman was preparing shredded linen to staunch the wounds, and *Pacha*, elevated to the dignity of doctor for the event, procured an instrument case, and put between a pair of pincers an enormous slug previously tainted red; the Blanquist and I drew straws to see who, who, who would be wounded (we sang it even). Fate fell on the youngest between us, that was me. I made a tear in my shirt, and I tainted my breast red, with a blackish dot in the middle.

The duel took place in fact at midnight. We took our places. The signal was given, I drew first... Someone had put powder into the pan, and the spark of the stone (our middle ages were in the stone age), with fire applied to it, produced a flash similar to a Roman candle, a silent flash – or *liquidium iodide*! – Naturally the Blanquist was not hit. It was frightening! he looked at me for a long time; "Fire already! fire!" someone said to him... He continued staring; finally he fired. Same flash of a Roman candle cut the black night... but I rolled on the ground, letting out inarticulate cries, holding convulsively my chest.

"There! there! That's it," I said.

Pacha, having thrown himself on me, was able to extract the slug in the dark, the slug with the pincers, all red... horror! he showed it to Camille who was alarmed.

I was rolling on the grass for a long time, then, tired of that exercise, I got it into my head to disappear. A hundred Hydropaths, returning from Bullier,[102] had attended this spectacle, and came to lend me a strong arm by way of help. I was almost torn to pieces.

The bearers feigned the greatest clumsiness, letting me fall from time to time. Camille shouted like the devil: "Be careful! is that how one treats a wounded man?"

They made him believe that he would be pursued. He went to consult with his uncle, who was a deputy. His uncle after having come to understand the affair in detail, was content to smile, telling him: "If someone pursues you, come back and see me!" And his uncle the deputy murmured dreamily: "Vague Luxembourg terrain! midnight! pistols from the middle ages! *liquidium iodide*!..."

That mystification was the last outburst of laughter for the phalanstery.

There were quite a few other more serious duels; but they had nothing to do with literature, and Corneille was not involved; I will not speak about them at all, no more than that splendid evening given by the Hydropaths at Bois-Colombes, that evening that no one who had been there is able to recall without being seized by a fit of laughter. These are the things that one acts out, and that cannot be written about.

How to explain that the Hydropaths, putting on a show at the Bois-Colombes, one never knew for whose benefit, missed the last train to Paris, remained prisoners in the theater, and began drinking. How innumerable disputes for no reason rose up despite the efforts of the president, the which, wishing to separate two combatants, pushed them towards a door which, opening brusquely onto a spiral

---

[102]Bullier: The Ball Bullier, a popular dance hall.

staircase, gobbled up into some oubliette the two fierce men: they fell into the obscurity, without harm, but without succeeding, before a good quarter of an hour, to make themselves known again. How fourteen duels were appeased, while an energumen was perpetually examining an almanac for the probable hour of sunrise, in order to kill at dawn an adversary whose name he didn't remember anymore... How the organizer of the small party was ignominiously shown the door... How Taboureux got back on the train on a dog's ticket and, disembarked in Paris, wanting to pay a visit at all costs to a notary friend of the family at around 7 o'clock in the morning... pure madness!

Never lock up fifty Hydropaths in a theater in the suburbs, or at least don't let them miss the last train.

From that epoch already so distant, I remember one singular evening when, returning in a white necktie and in the attire befitting the salon of a duchess, – yes, an authentic duchess – I had the bizarre idea to go and recite verse in a seedy dive on the rue Galande, where hard times had transformed Maurice Petit, ex-organist of the In-valids, into a humble accompanist of *flonflons*. I was nearly knocked out at first, then I became suddenly the friend of those people there, after having sang in their company and drank to their health. An-tithesis.

That was quite an unusual, dark, joyous and somber moment of existence. Having fallen really ill, I had to leave for the country-side, towards Fontainebleau, where my excellent friend Paul Marrot pulled I don't know what political card. There, I crushed the mi-crobes and was able to save myself from physiological misery. As for the anemic budget...

I climbed melancholily up, one evening, the incline of rue des Martyrs, paying a visit to the cabaret of the Grand'Pinte, where I hoped to tranquilize myself a bit while drinking with Manet, Des-boutins, and others. I was seated for several minutes when a joyful group made its entrance. They were several Montmartre Hydropaths: the painter René Gilbert, the giant Parizel, and this fellow, and that fellow; they came to sit next to me. All of a sudden, Gilbert said to me, while pointing out a young, strong man with reddish hair, who was with them:

"You know Rodolphe Salis?"

"No," I said. "Have you ever come to the Hydropaths."

"Never, I was painting in Cernay, far from the din of the city," responded the reddish-haired man.

And then, he added:

"I'm setting up an artistic cabaret at boulevard Rochechouart, 84, do you want to join us for the opening dinner?"

"Gladly," I replied.

And that's how I met Rodolphe Salis.

Chapter Eleven

The painter Salis. – The word of a father. – Founding the Chat Noir
*cabaret. – Description of the old cabaret on boulevard Rochechouart. –
The* Chat Noir *journal. – The voyageur A'Kempis. – Clément Privé, and
the sonnet* Because. *– Willette. – L'Institut. – The sessions. – The tumult.
– Parce Domine. – Death. – Maurice Rollinat. – Salis' pretend wake. –
King of Montmartre.*

Ah! Messeigneurs, gentlemen of the Butte, churls of the plain, bumpkins and tenant farmers, crossbowmen, mounted archers, and all others, ah! that cabaret that was at the beginning, the one that Rodolphe Salis founded!! Zounds! 'sblood! Son of a gun!

Salis was a painter and painted the stages of the cross for fourteen francs a piece! His father, a distiller-merchant from Châtellerault, hastened to curse him, him, the fine arts, and belle-lettres. Messeigneurs! that was a rude blow for Rodolphe: he tried to mollify his father, the inflexible father replied:

"Engage in commerce!"

At that time then, it was unusual to be opening medieval, Renaissance, or Louis XIII cabarets. The Grand'Pinte was of the same type; but there the painters got together without uproar, as if they were on the street. Salis thought of reintroducing the tumultuousness, the high madness, and the songs, iron-barded in our edulcorated mores. What's more, knowing quite well that all arts are brothers, he wondered why the literary types didn't rub shoulders with the painters, to lend them some fleeting syllables, perhaps ornamented with sonorous rhymes.

"I will be the gentleman cabaret owner," Salis said to himself, "still a painter, but also a litterateur and chansonnier. The future is mine!"

And the *Chat Noir* was founded.

Ah! Messeigneurs! That was a rude epoch when the L-shaped cat swung above the door, boulevard Rochechouart. I was there, grandma, I was there! We drank seriously, we sang to make the walls fall down, and sunrise saw us leaving that inauguration, noble and haughty, having finally become gentlemen of the middle ages – ah! no, not of the middle ages – but style Louis XIII, "The Most Pure," as Rodolphe said.

An L-shaped cat, on a stained-glass window, wooden tables, square, massive, solid seats (serving sometimes as ballistics against aggressors), enormous nails, called nails of *Passion* (the Passion of whom, O Louis XIII, the Most Pure)? tapestries stretched along the walls above the gleaming panels pulled off old chests (which Salis collected since his most tender childhood), a tall chimney, whose fate seemed later never to be lit, for it harbored under its mantel, carried on its andirons, all sorts of trinkets and curios: a warming pan, rutilant as if Chardin had painted it, an authentic skull (Louis XIII's perhaps), gigantic fire tongs, – a hotchpotch; but nary a log.

In a corner of the counter, a bust, *Le Femme inconnue*, from the Louvre, and, above it, an enormous head of a cat, surrounded by golden rays, as one sees in churches around the symbolic triangle. In the back, a second room, smaller, up three steps, had also at the height of a man's waist gleaming panels under the tapestries, on which the famous nails of the Passion supported stone rifles, useless swords, while the tall chimney – happily little like the other – replaced the antique bibelots by a quite modern and joyous stoked fire, around which a half-circle of painters and sculptors who stretched their legs and warmed their feet, who had come there from the beginning, and the feet also of poets and musicians, who weren't long to appear – following in the footsteps of the Hydropaths.

The opening of the cabaret took place in December, 1881. The presence of several poets brought about the birth of the *Chat Noir* journal in January 1882.

That was what made the gentleman Salis' cabaret immediately peerless. An illustrated journal, containing verse and prose, and announcements; this one, among others, from the first issue:

THE CHAT NOIR
CABARET LOUIS XIII
Founded in 1114 *by a fumist.*

It was in that same first issue that the announcement of the departure of the famous Montmartre reporter, A'Kempis (alias Émile Goudeau), for foreign countries denominated the United States of Paris. The idea of the free city of Montmartre was germinating.

A second explorer, Jacques Lehardy, departed also in another direction. This second voyageur was none other than the poet Clément Privé, the author of very pretty verse that cannot be found, and of a sonnet that many people claim to be author of.

There was a drawing by Salis in this issue.

Soon success responded to the calls. The illustrators appeared first: Willette, Pierrot-Willet, that poet of the pencil, the author of masterpieces of painting, such as *le Parce Domine, l'Enterrement de Pierrot,*[103] *le Vitrail* of the new *Chat Noir*, and countless designs like dramas or like comedies; for that there is the character of Willette's talent: an abstract conception dominating the composition, whose perfect form envelopes the idea, concretizes it, and renders it poignant: *les Oiseaux meurent les pattes en l'air, l'Age d'or,*[104] are as good as any poem. One has gotten out of the habit of thinking when looking at *bits* of painting; Willette, above all, wants to think and make think. He is melancholic most of the time, ironically sad; but sometimes a farcical gaiety grabs hold of him, or a satirical, pitiless verve, and then he's a master of laughter. He's called Will, like Shakespeare.

Tiret-Bognet, Henry Somm, Uzès, Henri Rivière, then much later Caran d'Ache and Steinlein were the titled suppliers of the *Chat Noir*. Tiret-Bognet, a humanitarian, a Salvationist, a soldier in the salvation army, sad and gentle; Henry Somm, a Parisianing lover of Japanese art, spiritual and gay; Uzès, satirical, taking silhouettes spryly; Henri Rivière, macabre, a sort of Rollinat of the pencil, who cast many a mortician in many a snowy passage; Caran d'Ache, the elegant illustrator, strait-laced, and Steinlein, illustrator of birds and cats, who also lifts little women's skirts.

---

[103] l'Enterrement de Pierrot: The Burial of Pierrot.

[104] *Les Oiseaux meurent les pattes en l'air, l'Age d'or: The birds die with their claws in the air, The Golden Age.*

And soon, from the vicinity of the Odeon, the poets and musicians hit the road for the *Chat Noir*. Rollinat, Haraucourt, Lorin, Paul Marrot, Charles Cros, Félicien Champsaur, Armand Masson, Georges Fragerolle, Léo Montancey, etc., etc., etc.

It was an invasion of those two arts: poetry and music, into the sanctuary of painting, in Montmartre, the land of plastic arts. There was, in front of the blazing fire in the small room in the back, a fusion between the diverse branches of Beauty. Also, it soon earned the nickname of The Institute, an ironic and gay nickname that stuck. The arrival of the poets and musicians led to the introduction of a piano, and little by little what one called the Friday sessions. That day then, around four o'clock, when a stormy crowd filled the benches inside and were leaning on tables loaded with drinking glasses, one saw, descending the three steps of the Institute with grave demeanor, as if they were descending the steps of the Acropolis, or the famous stones of Tortoni's at the very least, one saw the good speakers of sonnets and ballads, while, with a triumphal march, some heroic symphonist welcomed their approach.

Salis' voice rose up above the pipe smoke.

"Messeigneurs, silence, the celebrated poet X... will recite for you one of those poems for which crowns have been weaved by nymphs in grottos... in grottos of the holy city of Montmartre."

It was something of the sort, starting off grandly and coming to an abrupt end, or ending with some fine nonsense that that gentleman cabaret owner Rodolphe Salis' eloquence led him to speak.

With those resounding words, silence was established, and the young lyric poet poured out his stanzas of gold, silver, bronze, or nickle, that the dilettantes paid handsomely for in applause.

That was very quickly like a second hall of the Hydropaths, with this difference that in place of having students for the audience, it was painters, illustrators, and amateurs. Youth was in the majority; but one was not surprised, as one would have been in the Latin Quarter, at the sudden apparition of a white beard.

From the beginning, the journal was as fantastical, comical, and absurdly ironical as the poets were grave, choosing their darkest poems to read. I record the phenomenon unable to explain it. But soon the popular poet Jules Jouy appeared, as well as the cabaret singers Meusy and Mac-Nab, then Charles Leroy who, following in the footsteps of A. Pothey, imagined the military caricature of Ramollot, and that was absolutely like at the Hydropaths club, a blend – without doctrine – of gaiety and seriousness. From that moment to the present, I could rattle off the entire list almost of Hydropathic poets. Except for Taboureux, who remained inextricable on the rock of the Pantheon, like a chained Prometheus, all came to declaim their verse or publish them in the journal next to Willette's "poems."

The editor in chief, Émile Goudeau, had Edmond Deschaumes for sub-editor. The *Hydropath* journal was dead, *la Plume* (*la Revue verte*) dead also; the *Chat Noir*, journal, was the certain heir, just as the cabaret sessions were heir to the Hydropathic sessions.

But the acclimatization of the arts, so close to Élysée-Montmartre,[105] didn't happen all by itself. At first, the proprietor had asked Rodolphe Salis what sort of business he intended to run:

"Oh!" the gentleman cabaret owner responded, "this will be a very small cabaret-restaurant, for my friends, fifteen of us, very quiet folk... You'll see! you'll see!"

The proprietor could see perhaps; but, sure enough, he understood.

Zounds! Messeigneurs! The piano whined all day long, and in the evening, and into the deep of night; one sang in chorus the best refrains of popular repertoire, and sometimes one accompanied while tapping on zinc plates by way of gongs! Zounds! What quiet!

On several occasions, some horrible procurers attempted to come in and sit among us. Then the expulsions began; they came in numbers, and that ended with a formidable brawl... There was even a death!

But let's move on to a more happy topic.

---

[105]Élysée-Montmartre: a dance hall, concert hall, entertainment hall that opened in Montmartre in 1807.

The edifice – it was so Louis XIII – was long but narrow. Thirty people could fit in with difficulty, and when we were merely one hundred, it became one of those bizarre problems the happy solution of which science steps back in fright when faced with. The perpetual packing in! Sardines in oil!

An interior wall that was easy to knock down was all that separated us from the neighboring clockmaker. Why didn't that manufacturer cede his right to lease? Ah! the poor man! after having fallen into the hands of Sapeck, Alphonse Allais, and Louis Décori, it didn't take long for him to cry uncle.

We pushed back the limits of the cabaret, and on the conquered place, on the finally monopolized wall, Willette hung his large canvas: *Parce Domine*, which symbolizes in an arresting manner the simultaneously happy and atrocious life of the Troubadours of poetry and the Gobe-la-Lune pierrots. In a nutshell: from the Moulin de la Galette a strange procession descends towards an infernal river, towards a black river, the Seine, the collector of sewage. Young Pierrots, white and pink Pierrettes, in departure! Then, frenetic adolescents; then aging on the steep slope, always a glass in hand and a song on their lips, but carrying the bereavement of their illusions in their pallid faces, in dark colored clothing! Finally both collapsing, old faded Pierrot and Pierrette with crow's-feet, in a somber ditch, because of suicide doubtless, madness perhaps, or consumption, in a chasm where doleful sirens wait for their prey, while the Virtuous One, in a coffin decorated with a white cross, climbs into the sky where symbolic stars, eternally alert and joyous, dance.[106]

Sad page, wild advertisement by the poet Willette, who has the air of saying to the Villons scattered on the benches, next to the tables of the cabaret, and to the Bohemians who lift their glasses and shout their songs: "Brothers! Turn away before it's too late!"

That was the period when the idea of death haunted him, in the midst of comrades sparkling with audacious verve. He took pleasure in listening to Rollinat's macabre poems, ferocious cantilenas played to Baudelaire's darkest sonnets. Death attracts! Fortunately, some vibrant songs, some odes to Gaiety that we sang sometimes, chased away those funereal impressions, traces of which can be seen

---

[106] *Parce Domine*: a fragment of which painting is on the cover to this book.

in the drawing found in issue number 44 (*Chat Noir*, Saturday, November 11, 1882).

That then was the month precisely when the *Figaro*, under Wolff's quill, launched Maurice Rollinat into the limelight. The poet had his hour of very great success; the *Neuroses*, published by Charpentier, consecrated him definitively. He is the energetic bard of the lamentation of souls and of things. One cannot easily endure being perpetually submitted to that frightening torture of contemplating death face to face, and always sinking one's gaze into empty eye sockets; but Rollinat possesses an undeniable power to be able to pull it off, without falling into madness, and to return to us from that horrifying scene, his hair standing on end and his face completely destroyed, but his mouth still singing.

We too, more bizarrely audacious perhaps in our irony, we had dabbled with death. In order to force certain people who were harassing him to leave him alone, Salis resolved to have himself passed for dead. In spite of his family's supplications, it was decided, and here's how it was executed.

The *Chat Noir* journal appeared draped in mourning, with a funeral orison on that unfortunate gentleman, who, at his moment of success, had passed suddenly from life to death.

On the door, an enormous placard, bordered in black, bore this inscription: *Open for cause of death.* Rodolphe Salis himself represented the family, he was the brother of the deceased, a brother so resembling him that he seemed a twin almost.

On four chairs rested the violoncello case furnished by Tolbecque, a box covered in black cloth embroidered with silver tears; above, a round loaf of bread in the form of a crown; four candles were burning; in a tin can, a little water and an aspergillum. Then the friend D*** as master of ceremonies, the young painter S*** as a religious, G*** a simple bell ringer, agitating two metal trays against each other, imitating perfectly the sound of church bells.

When someone entered, he was asked to sit down, quietly. As soon as the cabaret was full, the discourse began. One person jeered at death, another slung mud at the cadaver, and Salis, hidden behind the piano, whispered to the orator: "Enough! enough!"

Some may find that of questionable taste, it was certain however that everyone who attended that funeral parody were unduly amused by it, with a nervous, special, irritating amusement, as if, at a wedding, after having drunk, one bawled in chorus some *dies irae* to a carnival tune. Schoolchildren and students are used to these lugubrious pleasantries. It's a privilege of youth. Now, we were young yet!

In less sad parody, there was the elevation of Salis to the grade of King of Montmartre. He had to dress in golden costume, extraordinary fabric, and hold a scepter. After having received the people's homage, he went out to take possession of the Moulin de la Galette. He betook himself there, hiding his royal vestments under an ulster, accompanied by painters and poets armed with halberds, who, all along the butte, to the astoundment of peoples, cried: "Long live the king!"

And we didn't get carted off to the police station.

It is true that *Grévy le Jurassique* was sung from time to time; and *Vive Grévy!*[107] so ironically albeit, compensated the seditious: "Long live the king!"

Some may take offense perhaps at my recounting this nonsense: basta! Life is not always so amusing that one should not reminisce on a time in the past that, honestly, was enjoyable, even if at the expense of the terrible Fates, and remind others that they have had their good quarters of an hour as well.

Then, after so many exploits of divers sorts, I profited from a beautiful opportunity to escape Montmartre for a while and go to the seashore, to put in order some scattered verse, which would make up the *Poèmes ironiques*.

---

[107]Grévy: Jules Grévy, President of the French Third Republic, AD 1879-1887.

Chapter Twelve

Jean Moréas. – New debutants. – Lutèce. – Decadents, instrumentalists, symbolists. – Quick assessment. – Le Courrier français. – The new Chat Noir. *– Shadowgraphs. – Shepherd in Asnières.*

On my return to the *Chat Noir*, I found a young man with a black mustache and a hook nose who wished to speak with me. His name was Jean Moréas, and he came to submit some verse for the journal. Of Greek origin, Jean Moréas was singing his fatherland at that time. Here's a piece that does not yet presage the revolutionary symbolist, but was from a poet without epithet:

> *EPODE*
>
> *I sing the burning summers, sultry summers,*
> *That ripen the climbing vines' dark grape,*
> *And precocious puberty's blossoming,*
> *I sing the summers of the vermillion Cyclades.*
>
> *Behind massifs of pine and elder*
> *Where, from the ancient portico, one sees*
> *Astragali couched in ripe wheat, oxen ruminate*
> *To the broken songs of chirping cicadas.*
>
> *All along tali planted with silver birch,*
> *Among rust thistles, prowling lizards*
> *Scintillating in the rays of crushing middays,*
> *Like the fine jewels of jasper and emerald.*
>
> *In the smiling valleys of Santorin island,*
> *Girls, with dark eyes garnished by long bangs,*
> *Along lost paths where the rosemary grows,*
> *Chase butterflies in orange corselets.*
>
> *And the proud vagabond with a disquieting eye,*
> *Sated by lubricious gypsies' bronzed breasts,*
> *On a bed of bracken, at a green pond's edge,*

Seeks a deep sleep in the plane trees' shade.

I sing the burning summers, sultry summers,
That ripen the climbing vines' dark grape,
And precocious puberty's blossoming,
I sing the summers of the vermillion Cyclades.

Jean Moréas, spoke these lines with a lilting voice in a strong Hellenic accent. He came assiduously to the *Chat Noir* and the *Hydropaths,* at their time of resurrection (of short duration).

Others as well debuted, on one or another of those *chariots of Thespis*: there was d'Esparbès, Jean Ajalbert, Darzens. Other young men such as René Ghill, F. V. Griffin,[108] Henri de Régnier, Morice got together in groups in the Latin Quarter, far from the Moulins de la Galette, near the old sacred Pantheon and noble Odeon; a new journal was founded, *Lutèce.* Georges Rall and Léo Trézenick improvised as printers, compositors even, page layout artists, correctors, to create with their hands that collection. They were a little aggressive against old comrades more or less "arrived" and, either by conviction or out of spite for competitors, they went and rediscovered Paul Verlaine, whom unjust fate had buried alive, and shined a light on Stéphane Mallarmé, who had no more need for it, it was felt, than, for example, the forgotten Raimbaud [sic]. Whatever! Since then, new leaders were found, not personalist leaders who said to everyone: Do as you like, provided you do it well! No, but the reconstitution of schools and coteries. The newcomers rallied around master Verlaine, or chief Mallarmé, and from there came the *Decadents* (of which the *Deliquescents* are nothing but parodists), the *Symbolists,* and the *Instrumentalists.* The very amusing parody by Adoré Floupette (Henry Beauclair and the poet Gabriel Vicaire[109]), the small opuscule entitled *Deliquescences,* was noticed by Paul Arène, who spoke for a long time about it in *Gil Blas.* That made the young decadents known. In the period of Roman decadence, there were lesser poets, *poetæ minores,* who used and abused

---

[108]F. V. Griffin: for examples of Griffin's excellent Symbolist poetry in English translation, see *Cull of April, Joys,* or *Swans* (Sunny Lou Publishing).

[109]Original footnote: Gabriel Vicaire just obtained the prize for the official *cantate* of 1889.

rhythms, alliterations, plays on words, convolutions, like Claudian, for example. Some Parnassian poets, holding them in high esteem, compared themselves to them. What's more, the word *decadent* implies, beyond affectation of style, a certain disorder fundamentally, a hybrid blend of old religions and refined mores; that was also what the decadents strived for; a particular sadism where Catholic incense is detected in loathsome places, and where the sanctuary has foul smells of face powder or even washbasin water.

Paul Verlaine, himself, is a true decadent. But the others, even more mysterious, grow distant through the grammatical forest, and borrowing his vagueness and his power of music, they transported it into the amplitude of phrases, into the modulation of rhythms, into the arrangement of words considered like simple notes in a score, like timbers in an orchestra, without their having a correspondence with any precise idea whatsoever other than sound. It was Stéphane Mallarmé and his loyal René Ghill, who wrote: *Legends of Soul and Blood*.

And then there are the Symbolists. The verb is not only a sound, it's a symbol, and the phrase, – not the phrase perhaps, – the flow is composed of words; the flow of words is a symbol; the poetry must give if not the comprehension, at least the apprehension, of intangible things, barely seen, that vanish quickly, far away. It is, if I understood it correctly, the system of Moréas and G. Kahn. And, on the ruins of *Lutèce* (the journal [not the city], hehe, no error!), they build, rather they *built* because today *The Independent Review*, the organ of the Symbolists, is the only journal that remains of that fuliginous melee. The talent abounds there. After permitted exaggerations, that school, like all schools taken with art, will produce its work. I sincerely hope so.

And, during this time, we others, their elders? Richepin has written volumes of prose and verse and has a drama in prose on the stage, a drama in verse, a comedy in verse, a comic opera. Maurice Bouchor, after having been unfaithful to poetry for so long a time in order to court music (oh! bigamy!), has just put out a volume of verse entitled *Symboles*, which provides a synthesis of ancient and modern cults, in bloom on the perduring terrain of the Ideal. Paul Bourget has said goodbye to verse and criticism, he's the fashionable novelist now, who was able to transport, without damage, the psychology of criticism into the living domain, and make it accepted by the masses. Maupassant holds on to glory by the right end of the stick. Raoul Ponchon has come down from his ivory tower and speaks in verse each week to readers of the *Courrier français*, that compilation where Willette leaves sometimes his signature, sometimes his velvet footprint, having for companions Henri Pille, Heidbrinck, Uzès, Lunel, Forain, while Jean Lorrain, the refined poet of *Modernities,* yammers on in lace jabot, while Mermeix brandishes the satirical whip, while Roger-Milès, director of the *Monde poétique*, a compilation of high merit, and Mauvrac offer a response under the severe eye of Jules Roques. Maurice Rollinat publishes both verse and songs. Haraucourt has just put out a novel, *The Friends*; Paul Marrot, a series of philosophical poems. Georges Moynet has published a very elaborate novel of studies, *Zonzon*. Champsaur writes ballets, Edmond Deschaumes resuscitates Gambetta, Charles Cros puts out here and there some pieces of verse.

There are those who have disappeared, and there are those who remain. The quasi-oceanic life of Paris ever bustles, turbulent tide, tempestuous sometimes.

And Salis, himself, has solicited the vote from his fellow citizens on two memorable occasions, through his now celebrated yellow bills: Here's one of his stupefying bills:

MUNICIPAL ELECTIONS OF MAY 4, 188*
XVIII ARRONDISSEMENT – MONTMARTRE QUARTER

VOTERS,

What is Montmartre? – Nothing!

What should it be – Everything!

The day has finally arrived when Montmartre can and must claim its autonomous rights from the rest of the city of Paris.

In fact, in its frequentation with that which we are accustomed to call the capital, Montmartre has nothing to gain but burdens and humiliations.

Montmartre is rich enough in finances, art, and spirit to survive on its own.

Voters!

Make no mistake!

Let's make the noble banner of Montmartre flap in the wind of independence.

"The Butte," that teat that has nourished Fantasy, Science, and all the truly French Arts, already has its organ: "The Chat Noir.*" From today forward, it must have its representative, a representative worthy of that name.*

RODOLPHE SALIS who, for three years now, directs, with the authority one knows, the Journal that is the joy of Montmartre, has appeared to us fit for that mission.

Montmartre deserves better than to be an arrondissement.

It must be a free and proud city.

Also, our program will be short and simple:

1. Separation of Montmartre from the State;

2. Nomination by the Montmartrois of a Municipal Council and a Mayor of the New City;

3. Abolition of octroi for the arrondissement, and the replacement of that vexatious tax by a duty on the Lottery, reorganized under the control of Montmartre, which will allow our quarter to provide for its needs and to aid the nineteen mercantile or poor arrondissements of Paris;

4. The protection of public alimentation. The protection of national laborers.

The Committee:

WILLETTE (Pierrot), 20, rue Véron.
POUSSARD (R. P. LaCayorne) 84, blvd. Rochechouart.
CHOUBRAQUE, rue Ramey, 38.
LEFÈVRE, rue Ramey, 38.
MARION, 26, rue Letort.
MARCEL-LEGAY, 92, boulevard de Clichy.
GERAULT-RICHARD, 44, rue des Abbesses.
DE SIVRY, 82, rue des Martyrs.
CATTELAIN (Ph.), 27, rue du Ruisseau.
RANDON, 82, rue des Martyrs.
COQUELIN (cadet), 84, boulevard Rochechouart.
JOUY (Jules)   —   —
ALLAIS (Alphonse)   —   —
LEROY (Ch.), man of letters, 23, boulevard Barbès.

Seen and Approved: RODOLPHE SALIS.

VOTERS,

This program will be defended with a fierce energy. –
I am one of those who would rather die than give up.

If I enter into the arena, you will see if my watch-
word, SERIOUS ALL THE SAME, is justified.

Voters, no abstention. Posterity awaits us.

Long live Montmartre!

Rodolphe SALIS
84, boulevard Rochechouart,
Candidate of Literary,
Artistic, and Social Demands.

Today, having transported his *Chat Noir* to rue Victor-Massé (previously rue de Laval), he inaugurated a new genre: the theater of shadowgraphs.

It's amusing and very artistic; it's signed both Caran d'Ache, as well as Willette or Rivière, Somm or Sahib.

In that décor of rue Victor-Massé (previously rue de Laval), the poets, such as the philosophical humorist Paul Marrot, such as the epically military chansonnier Ogier d'Ivry, such as Jean Rameau, the acclaimed author of the poem, *Life and Death*, Jean Floux, a very Parisian man, Armand Masson and other young and ardent men, having succeeded us, filling the entr'actes with magical shadowgraphs. Warrior odes follow *chansons d'amour* or flights into the blue. The rhymes ring, especially when Georges Fragerolle, having applied music to them, belts them out with his marvelous voice. Here's an excerpt from his compilation of verse, entitled *Chansons de France*, this one, the words of which were written by Paul Marrot:

> *The soldiers, on the highway,*
> *Head toward another garrison;*
> *It's beautiful weather out, one's had a drop;*
> *The sun rises on the horizon.*
>
> *The fold of the tunic floats*
> *In the matutinal breezes of spring,*
> *And the soldier, in his capote,*
> *Dreams of freedom in the fields*
>
> *Farewell, sentry boxes and barracks,*
> *Onward, all out of doors today;*
> *But other square barracks*
> *Are still there before him.*
> *Waiting for guard duty,*
> *He sings out loud in the air;*
> *All his campagnarde soul*
> *Vibrates with freedom in the fields.*
>
> *He sees, turned over in the plots,*
> *Plowshares like his own,*
> *And, on the solitary steeples,*
> *The weathercocks all look like his own.*
> *Above millstones upon millstones,*
> *The same setting suns;*
> *It's evening! all his thoughts*
> *Turn to freedom in the fields.*

The staging post is seldom extravagant,
The bivouac a sacred sojourn;
And one is quite tired
To learn how to fight one day...
Will we be, faces bruised,
Bowed down by harrowing canons?...
Onward! for the Fatherland,
And for freedom in the Fields.

I'd like to cite others, as well as certain, highly-attractive poetry; but I must speak of the chansonniers with the light and satirical
verve, who are none the less philosophical Parisians in their own
way: Jules Jouy, Meusy, and Mac-Nab. Meusy is a parodist of high-
sounding phrases; from him, this sentimental refrain:

Cheese! Poetry!
Hope of our meals,
What would life be like,
Without it.

Jules Jouy has a gay, macabre style, while Mac-Nab has
mournful gaiety. It's an amusing transposition. Here are two songs
that set the tone:

GUARDIANS OF THE PEACE

– To the tune of Canards
By Jules Jouy

When the sarges go out in ones,
That is, they're not with someone;
To better inspect, to better see,
In the same place 'til even,
They stand planted on the sidewalk,
Tralalala! Tralalala!

Refrain:

Peace! peace! peace! peace!

There they are: guardians of the peace!
Troulalaitou, latroulalaitou, latroulalaitou, latroulala!

Peace! peace! peace! peace!
There they are: guardians of the peace!
Troulalaitou, latroulalaitou, latrou...
Move on!

When the sarges go out in twos,
That is, they have someone to talk to;
The one says: "Me, I'm for Victor."
The other says: "Me, I'm for Chambord,
It's regrettable he's dead."
Troulalala (refrain)

When the sarges go out in threes
They're dressed as the bourgeoisie,
And that disguises them so well,
That under their new clothing,
One recognizes them immediately.

And that continues: *When the sarges go out in fours, it is to better see the winos fight, etc.; When the sarges go out in fives, it is to take little drinks on the zinc! etc.*

When the sarges go out in sixes
The bourgeois say: "It's the anarchiss!
What's going to happen, God in heaven!
T'is that ole fool de Louis' Michel
Who will climb back up his ladder!"

When the sarges go out in mass
They do whatever they please, it's none of your business,
Don't set a foot on the street.

For to put fear in the rioters,
They bang on the head of the rentiers.
Troulala, etc.
Move on

Mac-Nab earned his stripes as a chansonnier with *le Bal de l'Hôtel-de-Ville*, a fairly elaborate portrayal.

> *I arrive at the door of the ball*
> *I see the people one greets,*
> *It's all the municipal council,*
> *Standing in uniform:*
> > *Fully dressed in brown*
> > *And hats that are round,*
> *Damn! This ain't small potatoes;*
> > *All those chaps and chums,*
> > > *They've got it*
> *Just like* La Belle Jardinière.[110]

That Mac-Nab's seriousness is priceless. The poet Albert Tinchant, author of *Serenities*, accompanies him on the piano, unless he isn't standing in for the Baron B*** at the large cash register, charged with emphasizing the refrains *fortissimo*; what's more, he is the secretary of the *Chat Noir* journal, of which Alphonse Allais is the humoristic editor in chief. – N.B. Alphonse Allais resembles a clergyman.

It's a gay and macabre, gentle and warrior-like, spectacle, all at the same time, it's a full suit (but without the *La Belle Jardinière*, thankfully).

It's important that the Bohemians succeed one another but don't resemble one another; one generation has jovial Bohemianism, the following, a sad one; I have kind of an idea that the young Bohemians of the future will be more and more pessimistic: perhaps they have reason to be.

But we laughed heartily, I assure you; and when, after having become a colonist in Asnières[111] with an authentic shepherd guard dog, shepherd without sheep on the banks of the Seine, I take my walks, I think about the good ol' days sometimes, and I laugh still.

---

[110]La Belle Jardinière: a painting by Raphael.

[111]Colonist, in Asnières: apparently a lot of former French settlers from the Maghreb re-settled in Asnières.

That does not stop me from being pessimistic in my own way, noticing just how little real life resembles the dreams that one had at twenty. That makes me more serious, like a demoted prefect, and that is why I put a firm final stop here to TEN YEARS A BOHEMIAN.

FIN

Other Books by the Publisher

Fanchette's Pretty Little Foot
by Restif de La Bretonne,
translated by Richard Robinson

Je M'Accuse...
by Léon Bloy,
translated by Richard Robinson

My Hospitals & My Prisons
by Paul Verlaine,
translated by Richard Robinson

Salvation Through the Jews
by Léon Bloy,
translated by Richard Robinson

Words of a Demolitions Contractor
by Léon Bloy,
translated by Richard Robinson

Cellulely
by Paul Verlaine,
translated by Richard Robinson

Flowers of Bitumen
by Émile Goudeau,
translated by Richard Robinson

Songs for Her & Odes in Her Honor
by Paul Verlaine,
translated by Richard Robinson

On Huysmans' Tomb
by Léon Bloy,
translated by Richard Robinson

www.ingramcontent.com/pod-product-compliance
Lightning Source LLC
Chambersburg PA
CBHW031520120626
46545CB00005B/1921